Patience

Trusting God's Timing in Every Season

hope✳books collaborations

Chapter One: Patience: Learning to Walk When You Want to Run ©2026 by Dr. Tyann Beenken

Chapter Two: Adoption: Patience for God's Perfect Timing ©2026 by Stephanie A. Genrich

Chapter Three: Grace Tested: Dealing with Difficult People ©2026 by Marilynn Lester

Chapter Four: Divinely Orchestrated Love: It's Worth the Wait ©2026 by Lisa Recor

Chapter Five: Patience Came Through the Calm ©2026 by Kathleen Fischer

Chapter Six: Patience: Getting to the Joyful End ©2026 by Kelly Higdon

Chapter Seven: Patience: The Father I Found While Waiting for Her ©2026 by Jennifer Jackson

Chapter Eight: Letters to Timothy: Surrendering the Legacy to the God of the Long Wait ©2026 by Elizabeth Clark

Chapter Nine: Patience in Daily Life: Needing Patience in the Everyday ©2026 by Cathy Smith

Published by hope*books

2217 Matthews Township Pkwy
Suite D302
Matthews, NC 28105
www.hopebooks.com

hope*books is a division of hope*media

Printed in the United States of America

First edition.
Paperback ISBN: 979-8-89185-422-2
Hardcover ISBN: 979-8-89185-423-9
Ebook ISBN: 979-8-89185-424-6
Library of Congress Number: 2026938141

Table of Contents

Foreword

By Liz Caffman

*P*atience is one of the quiet strengths of the Christian life. It rarely announces itself with fanfare, yet it is woven through every season of growth, every unanswered prayer, and every moment when we are invited to trust God more deeply than our circumstances suggest. As one of the fruits of the Spirit, patience is not simply something we strive to manufacture through sheer willpower; it is something the Holy Spirit cultivates within us as we walk closely with Him.

This collaboration book was born from the understanding that patience is not learned in theory—it is formed in real life. It is developed in waiting rooms, in long nights, in uncertain transitions, in difficult relationships, and in seasons when progress feels slow or unseen. Each author in these pages brings an honest testimony of what it looks like to lean into God when answers do not come quickly and outcomes do not unfold as expected.

Patience stretches our faith in ways that comfort never could. It asks us to surrender control, release our timelines, and believe that God is working even when we cannot yet see the fruit. Through these stories, you will discover that patience is not passive; it is active trust. It is choosing peace over panic, faith over fear, and obedience over urgency. It is learning to rest in the assurance that God's timing is always purposeful and His plans are always good.

What makes patience such a beautiful aspect of the fruit of the Spirit is that it reminds us we are not alone in the process. The Holy Spirit walks with us in the waiting. He strengthens us when we feel weary and gently reshapes our perspective when frustration tempts us to rush ahead. Often, the very delay we resist becomes the place where God prepares our hearts for what is coming next.

Within these chapters, you will encounter stories of perseverance, surrender, healing, and hope. Some authors share moments of waiting for breakthrough, while others reflect on the slow work of transformation within their own hearts. Each testimony reflects a unique journey, yet together they reveal a common thread: God is faithful in every season, including the ones that require patience.

It is our prayer that as you read, you will feel encouraged in whatever season you are walking through right now. Whether you are waiting for direction, restoration, provision, clarity, or simply the strength to take the next step, may these stories remind you that waiting is never wasted when it is placed in God's hands.

May this collection help you see patience not as a burden, but as an invitation—an invitation to trust more deeply, to grow more fully, and to experience the peace that comes from knowing that God is always at work, even in the pauses.

May the Holy Spirit continue to produce His beautiful fruit within you, strengthening your heart and guiding your steps as you learn to wait well.

About the Chapters

Chapter One

This chapter uses the author's broken toe as a powerful metaphor for the spiritual lesson of slowing down and learning to trust God's timing. Through personal experience and biblical examples, including Lazarus, Joseph, Abraham, and David, the author demonstrates that delays are not obstacles but opportunities for growth, character development, and deeper faith. The chapter challenges the cultural pressure to hurry and strive, emphasizing that running ahead of God often creates turmoil, while surrendering to His timing produces peace. Ultimately, the author invites readers to walk with God at the "speed of love," trusting that His plans unfold perfectly in their proper season.

Chapter Two

This chapter shares the author's deeply personal journey through infertility and adoption, illustrating how patience and faith are essential when trusting God's timing. Through the biblical example of Sarah and her own adoption story, the author reveals how striving to control outcomes can lead to frustration, while surrendering to God's plan opens the door to unexpected blessings. After navigating delays, disappointments, and uncertainty, the author experienced God's perfect provision through the adoption of her son, affirming that waiting is never wasted when guided by faith. Ultimately, the chapter encourages readers to take the first step in obedience, trust God in the unknown, and believe that His timing will lead to the best possible outcome.

Chapter Three

In this chapter, Marilynn Lester shares personal experiences of parenting struggles, challenging classrooms, and painful relationships to illustrate how difficult people can test our patience and faith. She explains that true patience and unity cannot be achieved through human effort alone but come through the continual filling and guidance of the Holy Spirit. By yielding control to God, believers can respond with humility, forgiveness, and grace, even in the most trying circumstances. Ultimately, the chapter reminds readers that God often uses difficult relationships to transform our character, deepen our faith, and produce the fruit of the Spirit in our lives.

Chapter Four

In this chapter, Lisa Recor shares her deeply personal love story, revealing how God's perfect timing shaped her relationship through seasons of separation, growth, and renewed commitment. Through unexpected encounters, long-distance challenges, and spiritual transformation, she demonstrates that waiting on God strengthens faith, builds trust, and aligns hearts with His will. Her journey highlights that patience in love allows God to heal past wounds, deepen commitment, and orchestrate circumstances beyond human control. Ultimately, the chapter encourages readers to trust God fully, believing that what He prepares during the waiting is just as meaningful as the blessing itself.

Chapter Five

In this chapter, Kathleen Fischer recounts a life-altering diving accident that left her with a severe spinal injury, forcing her to navigate physical limitations, emotional hardships, and unexpected life changes. Through years of recovery, family challenges, and personal trials, she discovered that true patience often develops during seasons of stillness, uncertainty, and surrender. Her journey illustrates how faith, perseverance, and self-compassion can transform painful circumstances into opportunities for growth and renewed purpose. Ultimately, the chapter encourages readers to trust God through life's storms, recognizing that patience cultivated in hardship can lead to strength, healing, and deeper understanding.

Chapter Six

In *Patience: Getting to the Joyful End*, Kelly Higdon shares a deeply personal journey of faith shaped through unexpected hardship while serving at a missionary boarding school in Côte d'Ivoire during political unrest and tragedy. Through seasons of uncertainty, loss, and redirection, she discovered that patience is not merely waiting, but trusting in God's presence, provision, and greater purpose even when the path is unclear. Her story reveals that patience is a fruit of the Spirit formed through surrender, allowing God to transform suffering into spiritual growth and deeper dependence on Him. Ultimately, patience becomes the pathway that leads believers to hope, healing, and the joyful assurance of God's eternal promises.

Chapter Seven

In *Patience: The Father I Found While Waiting for Her*, Jennifer Jackson shares a powerful testimony of overcoming deep wounds from a painful relationship with her mother and the absence of her earthly father. Through years of spiritual struggle, surrender, and healing, she discovered that patience is not passive waiting but an active trust in God's transforming work. As she allowed God to become the Father her heart longed for, He restored her identity, softened her heart, and gradually brought healing to her family relationships. Ultimately, her story reveals that patience, rooted in surrender to God's higher ways, opens the door for restoration, freedom, and the fulfillment of His promises.

Chapter Eight

In *Letters to Timothy: Surrendering the Legacy to the God of the Long Wait*, Elizabeth Clark vulnerably shares the long journey of trusting God with her son's future after a traumatic car accident altered the course of their lives. Through heartfelt letters, she wrestles with fear, guilt, control, and the painful tension between a parent's hopes and God's timing, ultimately learning the difference between patience for circumstances and long-suffering love for people. As she releases her expectations and surrenders her son's story to God, she discovers that faithful prayer and trust become the pathway for healing, growth, and redemption. This chapter reminds readers that even in seasons of silence and delay, God continues His work, shaping both parent and child for His greater purpose.

Chapter Nine

In this chapter, Cathy Smith reflects on the essential role of patience in navigating both life's ordinary challenges and major trials, including her own painful experiences with divorce and betrayal. She emphasizes that patience is an active endurance, requiring self-control, trust in God's timing, and perseverance through emotions, conflicts, and uncertainty. Through personal anecdotes—from waiting during pregnancy to managing everyday frustrations—she illustrates how patience is intertwined with other virtues such as love, gentleness, and faithfulness. Ultimately, Cathy encourages readers to seek God's guidance, remain calm in difficult situations, and cultivate patience as a spiritual discipline that shapes character and strengthens relationships.

Chapter 1

Patience: Learning to Walk When You Want to Run

By Dr. Tyann Beenken, DPT

"YOU WILL NEVER BE ABLE TO DESIGN ANYTHING BETTER THAN WHAT HE HAS FOR YOU. LAY IT ALL DOWN AND LET HIM LEAD!"
-SOMER PHOEBUS[1]

RACK! I heard it. I felt it. I knew it.

I had been carrying my three-year-old, practically running down our stairs, hurrying to get everyone out the door and on to the next thing. Then, I slipped off the edge of the step. With my daughter balanced in one arm, I quickly reached out to grab the railing with the other to keep from falling down the stairs. In doing so, I landed awkwardly on the next step, and my right foot crumpled under our combined weight. Thankfully, she was not hurt at all; I was a different story. The sound and the pain in my foot gave it away. The X-ray confirmed what I already knew. My big toe was broken in multiple places.

This was my first broken bone, and while a broken toe may not seem like a major injury, your big toe serves a pretty significant function in walking/running. I had been training to run a race that summer, and without the ability to extend my big toe and push off of it, I was done running for a while. This was a setback I did not have time for.

Once the bone was healed, it would take even more time to restore the mobility needed for proper walking/running mechanics. I was very frustrated. I wanted to run but was stuck walking for a while, and walking felt like settling. It felt slow. It felt too easy. It felt like missing out and being left behind while everyone else continued to push ahead. But I also knew that if I rushed the healing process and returned to running too soon, I could cause further stress and injury, not just to my foot, but to the rest of my body. So, I walked. And in the slower pace of walking, God met me and began to show me things I had missed while running.

Metaphorically speaking, I had been running from one thing to the next for many years, pushing the limits of what I could handle: running my physical therapy practice, raising a growing family, homeschooling, and trying to juggle all the demands and responsibilities of work, home, and my own spiritual walk. I felt like I was on a treadmill that kept going faster, and I was struggling to keep up. On the outside, everything looked fine. I had it all and was "successful" in the eyes of the world. But on the inside, I was crumbling under the weight of responsibility and expectation. Something had to give, or I was going to break, and not just my toe.

God made it clear to me that I needed to let the physical therapy practice go. Even as the doors to my business closed, I sensed that God was going to do something new, something different. Isaiah 43:18-19 (ESV) kept coming to my mind:

> Remember not the former things, nor consider the things of old. Behold, I am doing a new thing; now it springs forth, do you not perceive it?...

I believed God was urging me to let go of the past and my "old" business and to look forward to what He was going to do next. A new dream and a new vision for my practice began to form in my heart and mind, and I started to run towards it. As I took off in the direction of new ideas, new goals, and new deadlines, I kept tripping. Things were not falling into place, and I was discouraged. If God had given me this new dream, why wasn't it coming to fruition? Had I been wrong? Had I misunderstood God's leading?

As I wrestled with these questions, God began to show me the answer. I was sprinting ahead of His timing. Yes, the dream was good, but the timing was not.

Our culture conditions us to want what we want and want it now. The thought of having to wait, or even say "no," creates a sense of anxiety and restlessness that we do not quite know how to manage in our instant access, instant gratification world. In order to be "successful," we are told to hustle after goals—to work harder, faster, and longer. In the guided journal that accompanies her book *Present over Perfect*, Shauna Niequist writes about this chase for success, saying:

> "We sometimes forget there's more than one way to steward a calling. We don't have to pursue bigger and faster."[2]

The fear that there will not be space or opportunity for us later causes us to rush forward, saying "yes" to every opportunity that crosses our path, whether it's the right thing or not. If you wait, you lose. That is a scarcity mindset, and our God is the God of abundance. His kingdom operates in a different way, and He is not bound by the constraints of time.

> For my thoughts are not your thoughts, neither are my ways your ways, declares the Lord. 'For as the heavens are higher than the earth, so are my ways higher than your ways and my thoughts than your thoughts.
>
> Isaiah 55:8-9, ESV

In his book, *The Ruthless Elimination of Hurry*, John Mark Comer has much to say about the speed at which we live and our pursuit of bigger and faster. He contrasts our frenetic pace with that of Jesus, who, though He was very busy here on Earth, was never in a hurry. He did not run from place to place. He walked. Comer writes, "Hurry and love are incompatible." He goes on to note that the first word to describe "love" in 1 Corinthians 13:4 is "patient," and then says, "There's a reason people talk about 'walking' with God, not 'running' with God. It's because God is love."[3]

God met me walking as my toe was healing, and He has met me here in this season of waiting. My default speed is to hurry and run as fast as I can, but God also has a speed. His speed is love, and love is patient.

So, I am learning to walk with Him, instead of running ahead of Him.

And as I walk with Him, He is teaching me:

- His timing is greater than mine
- Delays serve a purpose
- Striving creates turmoil
- Surrender brings peace

Let's look at four Biblical examples and consider what the stories of these men and women—Lazarus and his sisters, Joseph, Abraham, and David—teach us about patience, God's timing, and His ultimate purpose.

God's Timing > Our Timing

In John chapter 11, we read an interesting account of Jesus. He has recently learned that one of His dearest friends, Lazarus, is ill. His sisters, Mary and Martha, have sent for Him, but Jesus says to His disciples in verse 4 (ESV), "This illness does not lead to death. It is for the glory of God, so that the Son of God may be glorified through it." One might expect Jesus to rush off to heal His friend, but Jesus does something completely different. Jesus stays where He is for two more days! Then He and His disciples go to Lazarus's home in Bethany, where Lazarus has since died. As they were walking to Bethany, Jesus said to His disciples, "For your sake, I am glad that I was not there, so you may believe." (John 11:15, ESV).

As He nears their home, Martha comes out to meet Jesus, confronting Him, saying, "Lord, if you had been here, my brother would not have died." (John 11:21, ESV). Jesus then goes on to have a very poignant and profound conversation with Martha about life and death. He tells her in John 11:25-26 (ESV), "I am the resurrection and the life.

Whoever believes in me, though he die, yet shall he live, and everyone who lives and believes in me shall never die. Do you believe this?"

When He reaches the tomb of Lazarus, Jesus asks for the stone to be moved. Martha objects, as it has now been four days since Lazarus died. Jesus commands Lazarus to come out of the tomb, and Lazarus walks out! In this instance, we might ask, "God, why the delay?" "Why wait?" "Why not go and heal Lazarus right away?"

We have the benefit of reading Scripture and knowing how the story ends. Jesus knew what would happen and what He would do, but Mary, Martha, and the disciples did not. The disciples did not understand why Jesus waited. Mary and Martha were frustrated and hurt. Jesus did not come right away, and their brother died. They did not understand the purpose behind the delay.

If Jesus had gone and healed Lazarus as soon as He had heard of his illness, the disciples, Mary, and Martha would have seen Jesus heal Lazarus, but they already knew Him as a healer. In the delay and subsequent death and resurrection of Lazarus, they learned something far greater...they came to know Jesus as the One who could not only heal the living, but raise the dead.

Like Mary and Martha, we may not understand God's timing when we find ourselves in a season of waiting. But as we wait on God, we will come to know Him in a deeper way, and we will find that He has high and holy purposes in the delays.

Delays Serve a Purpose

As a young man of 17, Joseph had a dream that he would one day rule over his father and brothers, and they would bow down to him. Joseph's brothers, who were already jealous of him, became even angrier when Joseph told them of his dream, and they sold him into slavery. Joseph ended up in Egypt as a servant of Potiphar, and after a false accusation, was thrown into prison. While in prison, Joseph, with the help of God, accurately interprets the dreams of two prisoners. Joseph asks one of the prisoners to remember him and to present his case to Pharaoh, the ruler of Egypt. The prisoner is restored to his former position, but forgets about Joseph, and Joseph remains in prison for another two years. At this point, Pharaoh himself has a dream that no one can interpret. The former prisoner remembers Joseph and tells Pharaoh about him. Joseph is released from prison and comes before Pharaoh. Again, with God's help, he accurately interprets Pharaoh's dream. At 30 years old, Joseph rises to power, second only to Pharaoh. The dreams he had as a teenager finally came true when, through the circumstances of famine, his brothers came down to Egypt to buy food and bowed down before Joseph (Genesis 42).

As a teenager, Joseph was not mature enough, nor initially equipped for the task God had in store for him. He had much to learn and a lot of growing up to do before he was ready to lead and rule others. In Genesis chapter 39, we read multiple times that "the Lord was with Joseph" during his time of imprisonment in Egypt. During those years of trial and hardship, God transformed Joseph from an arrogant adolescent into a humble, mature, and wise leader, who was able to forgive his brothers and say to them, "As for you, you meant evil against me, but God meant it for good, to bring it about that many people should be kept alive, as they are today," (Genesis 50:20, ESV).

In the 13-session companion study guide to *Experiencing God: Knowing and Doing God's Will*, Henry Blackaby writes:

> God uses the smaller assignments to develop character. God always builds character to match His assignment. If God has a great task for you, He will expand your character to match that assignment.[4]

Joseph was given a very large assignment. He was used in a mighty way to preserve the nation of Israel when famine struck. At 17, he was not ready for the assignment, but 13 years later, at age 30, he was. God needed to develop Joseph's character and mature his faith before he was ready to be used by Him to complete the tasks ahead.

Like Joseph, could God be using a season of waiting or trial as a time of preparation in your life? Maturing your faith and developing your character to fit the task ahead? Are you willing to give Him the time He needs to do just that?

Waiting can be hard, but running ahead of God's timing is costly.

Striving Creates Turmoil

It is hard to wait for something we want. If we have been waiting a long time, the temptation to take matters into our own hands, to "help" God by moving things along ourselves, becomes stronger. Doubt creeps in, fear of missing out builds, and in the world's eye, we are justified to jump ahead. But when we go outside of God's boundaries and run ahead of His timing, trying to make things happen in our own strength, we create stress and turmoil, not just in our own lives, but in the lives of others as well.

In his book, *Experiencing God: Knowing and Doing God's Will*, Henry Blackaby writes, "Doing things God's way is always best."[5] He goes on to say that "with God, *how* you do something is as important as *what* you do. It is possible to do the right thing in the wrong way or at the wrong time."[6] Malinda Fuller echoes this sentiment in her book, *Obedience Over Hustle*, saying, "The right thing, at the wrong time, is the wrong thing."[7]

One of the clearest examples of this principle is the story of Abraham. Abraham desired the right thing (a son), but ran ahead of God's timing. As a result, he and his family suffered the consequences when they went about things in the wrong way.

In the book of Genesis, back when he was still called 'Abram,' Abraham was chosen to be the father of the nation of Israel. He was 75 years old when he left his home country and followed God to a new land. When he and his family arrived in Canaan, God promised to make him into a great nation and to give the land to Abraham's descendants. God promised Abraham that He would have his very own son. However, this promised son was not born right away, nor was he born the following year.

Ten years had gone by, and still, Abraham's wife, Sarah (Sarai), had not conceived a child. In Genesis 16, growing impatient for this promised child, Sarah gives Abraham her servant, Hagar, to be his wife and produce an heir for them. Hagar conceived and bore Abraham a son named Ishmael. This created a lot of turmoil and stress within their family unit at the time. Thirteen years later, the turmoil only increased when Sarah gave birth to God's promised son, Isaac. Abraham was 100 years old when Isaac was born, and this was more than 20 years after God had first given the promise! Much pain and heartache could have been avoided had Abraham continued to surrender the fulfillment of the promise and his fears to God instead of striving to make things happen on his own.

Like Abraham, I have been impatient for God to move. After I closed my practice, I assumed God would open all the doors to the new business idea I had, and it would just take off. But it didn't. When it stalled, I pushed harder. I gave in to the fear that I would miss out. I believed the lie that if I didn't make this happen now, there wouldn't be space or opportunity for me later. All my efforts, all my striving to make things happen, left me feeling stressed, overwhelmed, and burned out. I wasn't the only one who felt the effects–my family suffered along with me.

In the book, *She Works His Way: A Practical Guide for Doing What Matters Most in a Get-Things-Done World,* Michelle Myers writes, "Striving says, 'I've got this.' Surrender says, 'God's got me.'"[8] It wasn't until I stopped long enough to realize what I was doing–running ahead of God and trying to make things happen on my own that I began to sense God was asking me to lay this new dream down as well. It was not for "now," but for "later." I needed to trust Him with the timing. A striving heart believes it all depends on her. A surrendered heart knows it all depends on God. And that knowledge brings peace and sets one free.

Surrender Brings Peace

David, the second king of Israel, did not immediately succeed to the throne after he was anointed. We are told in 1 Samuel 15 that because of Saul's (the first king of Israel) disobedience to God's commands, the throne would be taken from Saul and given to another. Samuel, the prophet and priest at that time, was sent to the house of Jesse to anoint one of his sons to be the next king. Jesse's sons paraded in front of Samuel, yet not one of them was the one God had chosen to be king. Samuel asked if Jesse had any more sons, and the youngest, David, who was out watching the sheep, was brought before Samuel. As David entered, the Lord spoke to Samuel, saying in 1 Samuel 16:12 (ESV), "Arise, anoint him, for this is he."

We are not told exactly how old David was when he was anointed as the next king, but most references place him between the ages of 10 and 15 years old. Later, in 2 Samuel 5:4 (ESV), we read that "David was thirty years old when he began to reign." What happened during the 15-20 years between David's anointing and his becoming king?

From 1 Samuel 17-2 Samuel 5, we read about the triumph and turmoil of David's life, from his victory over Goliath to running for his life from Saul. In 1 Samuel 26, we find Saul chasing David again. During the night, David and Abishai come into Saul's camp while he is sleeping, and Abishai offers to kill Saul. David responds, "Do not destroy him, for who can put out his hand against the Lord's anointed and be guiltless?" (1 Samuel 26:9, ESV). David could have taken Saul's life to become king himself. Instead, he chose to honor and obey God, not to lift his hand against God's anointed, but instead to wait for God's timing.

Throughout the Psalms, many of them penned by David himself, we are encouraged to "wait on the Lord." This waiting implies a firm trust and confident hope in God. David writes in Psalm 27:14 (ESV), " Wait for the Lord; be strong, and let your heart take courage; wait for the Lord. And in Psalm 25:3 (ESV), David says, "Indeed, none who wait for you shall be put to shame." In the years between his anointing and the start of his reign, David walked with God, seeking Him, and surrendering to His plans. God, in turn, transformed a young, inexperienced shepherd boy into one of the greatest kings of Israel.

When God gives us a job to do or a dream for the future, He rarely lays out all the steps or gives us the whole plan. Instead, He asks us to simply trust Him with one step at a time. As we take one faithful step, He continues to show us the next step and the next step. In all situations and circumstances, God is seeking a relationship *with* us, not performance or achievement *from* us. The more we know who God is, the more we will trust Him. The more we know and trust Him, the easier it is to follow Him. Peace does not come from having everything perfectly planned out. Peace comes from knowing and trusting the One whom we are following.

This peace enabled Abraham to lay his promised son, Isaac, on the altar when God asked him to in Genesis 22. This peace allowed David to wait on God's timing as he was chased by Saul. It also allowed him to pass on his dream of building a temple, when God told him it was not for him to do, but for his son, Solomon, to accomplish in 1 Chronicles 17. This peace empowered Jesus Christ to submit Himself to God's plan for our redemption, praying in the Garden of Gethsemane, "not my will, but yours, be done," in Luke 22:42-43 (ESV).

God's ultimate purpose in all things is to draw us into a deeper knowledge and understanding of who He is, and in doing so, conform us into the image and likeness of His Son, Jesus Christ. In each of the instances above, the delays served to grow character, deepen faith, and develop a spiritual maturity that equipped them for their calling.

Friends, I do not write these things lightly, or because I have figured out the secret of patience. I write these things because this is my struggle...this is what God has been teaching me and showing me over the last few years.

I was that working mom who had run herself ragged trying to do and be all the things God called her to be as a wife and mother, while at the same time trying to be and do all that the world expected of her as an entrepreneur and business owner. Chasing every opportunity for fear of missing out. I laid one business down on the altar only to start running towards a new dream and a new vision for my professional career. But God has asked me to lay that on the altar, as well. It's hard to surrender and lay down a dream you feel God has given you, especially when you see others around you pushing ahead and achieving those very things. Every time I am tempted to pick it up again and run with it, He whispers to my heart, "Wait. It's not time to pick it up yet. We still have some training to do before you run, and I have a different job for you to do now, in this season. Trust Me for the "more" later."

Somer Phoebus writes in *She Works His Way: A Practical Guide for Doing What Matters Most in a Get-Things-Done World*, "You will never be able to design anything better than what He has for you. Lay it all down and let Him lead!"[9] And so, I am learning to walk with God at the speed of love, following His lead instead of running ahead of Him, and finding peace and freedom in the surrender.

> "Now to him who is able to do immeasurably more than all we ask or imagine, according to his power that is at work within us, to him be glory in the church and in Christ Jesus throughout all generations, forever and ever! Amen."
>
> Ephesians 3:20-21

Journal & Prayer Prompts:

Sometimes we have a clear vision of what God is calling us to. At other times, it may seem a little fuzzy. When the vision is clear and the goals attainable, it is easy to charge ahead. But we need to seek God first, asking Him if this is something for right now or in the future. Even though the vision may be clear, the timing could be wrong. If He says, "wait," it could be that He has something else for us to do now.

1. What current dreams/goals do you have for your life?

2. Think of a traffic signal where green means go, yellow means proceed with caution, and red means stop. Is God giving the goals you wrote above a green light, a yellow light, or a red light in your current season?

3. If God is giving you a yellow light or a red light:

   a. What might He want to teach you, or what might He want you to focus on in this season?

   b. What thoughts, attitudes, or beliefs do you have that could be causing you to run ahead of God's timing?

4. If God is giving you a green light, what thoughts, attitudes, or beliefs do you have that could be holding you back?

5. Read the following Scripture passages:
   - Psalm 27:14
   - Psalm 37:3-7
   - Proverbs 3:5-6
   - Psalm 46:10
   - Isaiah 46:10
   - Ephesians 3:20-21
   - Philippians 1:6

In light of the challenge to patiently wait on the Lord and His timing, what do you notice in these verses?

Abba Father, I confess my own impatience and desire to run ahead of Your timing. I acknowledge I am short-sighted and my knowledge is limited, but You see the end from the beginning, and everything in between. In your presence is fullness of joy. At your right hand are pleasures forevermore. You are the God of abundantly more than I can ever ask or imagine. Lord, you know the desires and motives of my heart. Mold them until they align with Yours. Give me the courage to wait patiently for Your timing, but give me the boldness to move forward when You say, "Go." In the wait, help me trust that because You love Me, Your plans for me are good, and Your timing is perfect. Amen.

Chapter 2

Adoption: Patience for God's Perfect Timing

By Stephanie A. Genrich

CONSIDER IT PURE JOY, MY BROTHERS AND SISTERS, WHENEVER YOU FACE TRIALS OF MANY KINDS, BECAUSE YOU KNOW THAT THE TESTING OF YOUR FAITH PRODUCES PERSEVERANCE. LET PERSEVERANCE FINISH ITS WORK SO THAT YOU MAY BE MATURE AND COMPLETE, NOT LACKING ANYTHING. IF ANY OF YOU LACKS WISDOM, YOU SHOULD ASK GOD, WHO GIVES GENEROUSLY TO ALL WITHOUT FINDING FAULT, AND IT WILL BE GIVEN TO YOU. BUT WHEN YOU ASK, YOU MUST BELIEVE AND NOT DOUBT, BECAUSE THE ONE WHO DOUBTS IS LIKE A WAVE OF THE SEA, BLOWN AND TOSSED BY THE WIND. THAT PERSON SHOULD NOT EXPECT TO RECEIVE ANYTHING FROM THE LORD.

JAMES 1:2-7

"I want to face trials, hardships, and long swaths of time spent just waiting for answers to my greatest questions in life," said no one *ever*. No, we are the instant gratification society of our day. Where finger tapping and eye rolls take place while waiting for the microwave to "ding" with your finished minute cup of soup. Waiting is not in our nature. Even with great fortitude and discipline, it's difficult for us to rein in our urge not to seek immediate gratification. Yet the wisdom of life experience reminds us that God's very best is in his timing and not ours. Corralling our impatient need for answers is necessary if we are to follow God's will and not our own preconceived plan.

A few years after having our first child, my husband and I were ready to commit to expanding our family. The only problem was - nothing happened. I was 41 years old. Not at the height of my reproductive years, but not entirely out of the question either. After a year of following my body rhythms, cycles, and taking drugs (which apparently altered my demeanor to more of a Dr. Jekyll and Mr. Hyde persona, or so I'm told), still nothing happened. Further testing revealed I was, in fact, in the perimenopause stage of aging. That diagnosis blindsided me. With no family history to say otherwise, I had clearly not anticipated this result. I loved being pregnant with our daughter. No morning sickness, I had felt great, minus the 60+ pounds I had gained and then lost. Some grieving needed to take place in the aftermath of this devastating news. We slowly began to process and understand that we were living with a new reality. *How did God want us to proceed? Should we continue down the path of expanding our family, or was this a hard "no" coming from God?*

Surrender to self: Be committed to God's will over your own

As with any trial in life, we all have a choice to make. Am I going to be focused on what it is that I want, above all else, or will I seek God's will in the midst of my ordeal? The latter of the two invariably requires a commitment to patience, because patience is all about God's timing and not our schedule.

Have you ever had a desire or dream that you feel was stomped out for one reason or another? Or did you simply perceive it as a temporarily blocked road? One is immovable, while the other may still have a glimmer of light at the end of the tunnel. That tunnel might be very long with twists and turns coming at you from all sides. But all you need is the hope from God's light to keep our dream alive. Are you willing to latch onto that light and commit to your dream? I mean, really commit, because more than anything, it will undoubtedly require fortitude along with a lot of patience to get you to the end.

Genesis 16 tells a story of Sarah, a woman desperately longing for a child of her own. Since she is elderly and well past childbearing years, Sarah decides to take matters into her own hands. Maybe she thought God wasn't moving fast enough and needed her help to get things rolling. Sarah comes up with a plan to have her husband, Abraham, sleep with her maidservant Hagar, and thereby conceive a child with Hagar, whose baby Sarah would then take as her own to raise–not a good idea.

In Sarah's desperate attempt to have a child, she is blind to the repercussions her actions will produce. Yet her unwillingness to wait and be patient led to her overzealous choices with lasting effects. My only guess is that in Sarah's mind, this was a great way to get what she wanted. However, human emotions are the same today as they have been for thousands of years. Envy, contempt, and jealousy created a large wedge that grew between Sarah and Hagar. Once Hagar was able to provide Abraham with a child, resentment and strife fueled by pride bubbled up within Sarah. This led to a fracture in the relationship among all three. The forthcoming baby boy, Ishmael, was not embraced by Sarah as her son but instead remained with Hagar.

Sarah must have been skeptical about her ability to ever become a mother at this point. It's difficult to change course once our mind is set on a specific desire and the path we think we need to take to get there. Particularly when that dream is as emotionally charged as motherhood. Having already experienced the birth of my first child, I assumed we were on a 'rinse and repeat' cycle with our next addition. My mind was as narrowly focused as Sarah's had been. At first, we both thought we had a great plan on how to welcome a son. Mine was through childbirth, and Sarah's was through employing her maidservant. Different means leading to the same outcome.

When we surrender to ourselves and get out of our own way, we see God's plan more clearly. But in order to do this, we must be patient with ourselves and God. This type of patience is rooted in having *faith in the in-between.* I have been known to be a bit of a control freak. Maybe you are too. We like to have a plan that is mapped out from beginning to end with all the possible deviations accounted for ahead of time. Yes, in my perfect world, this is how life works, but my world isn't perfect, and I'd bet yours isn't either. No, we live in reality where freedom of choice rules, per God's will. This brings with it loads of opportunities to practice having patience, with ourselves, with others, and with God.

It took a while for the numbness to slowly turn into acceptance of our new normal. If we were ever going to expand our family, it was not going to happen as it did before. Were we willing to look at other options?

Patience: fueled by the strength of faith

While getting ready for work one December day, the show *Good Morning America* was on in the background. Steven Curtis Chapman, a contemporary Christian singer, was telling the story of his daughter's tragic death.[1] He and his wife, Mary Beth, had added three daughters to their family through international adoption from China. The youngest of these, Maria Sue, was accidentally killed in the family's driveway. The Chapmans briefly explained their journey through international adoption. This story touched my heart so deeply while simultaneously turning on a lightbulb. Like Sarah, I thought I had a great idea.

Growing up, some of my closest friends had been adopted, so I had a very positive perception of adoption. It just had never really crossed my mind as a serious consideration. For the first time, I knew, without a shadow of a doubt, this was the path God wanted us to take. This "knowing" had only happened a couple of times in my life. It's a rock steady awareness within yourself. Not an emotional feeling per se, but knowing which direction is true North. The direction of God's plan for you. It's a gift to be given this present of mind and something that only happens, in my experience, after an enormous amount of prayer. Have you ever experienced this undeniable gift of "knowing"? If not, keep leaning into God for his guidance. Ask Him to show you the plan He has for the answers you seek.

My husband, Greg, had similar experiences with childhood friends who found their way to forever families through adoption. We had a lot of discussions between the two of us and as a family with our daughter, on how we felt about starting this process. More than anything, we stayed in constant prayer. Adoption felt scarier than childbirth, mainly because 99% of it is out of your control. This was going to be a big step for our faith and patience.

Also, where do you start? There are so many roads that can lead to a potential placement. So many legalities to navigate, agencies to choose from, and requirements to fulfill that the process was overwhelming. International adoption, as the Chapmans chose, had additional requirements depending on the country, and these requirements were all over the board. The Hague Convention of Intercountry Adoption[2] provides some measure of standards and consistency that most countries open to adoption outside their borders follow.

After spending over a year in meetings with international adoption agencies, learning how to navigate this complicated web, we were no closer to being able to start the actual process. It was at this time that events happened that placed a dark shadow over Americans adopting from foreign countries, particularly countries we were considering: China, Guatemala, and Russia. Therefore, a temporary hold was in place on American adoptions until such a time that bad players could be filtered out and processes refined. A completely understandable reaction when precious lives are at stake. However, this new revelation placed a reset on our entire plan. Adoption is a long process. Had we missed our child because of the length of time spent on paperwork and protocol?

Up to this point, I had been fairly patient, but the gloves were coming off. Time was ticking. Neither of us was getting any younger. A fact we were consistently reminded of at every adoption meeting. A few countries had already refused to consider us based on our age. I didn't think I could feel any older than when my doctor referred to me as a "geriatric mother" while I was pregnant with my daughter, but guess what? I did. Not a confidence booster for any mom. On the bright side, we had passed the BMI (Body Mass Index) requirements imposed by a few countries.

Had we wasted crucial time spinning our wheels on paperwork and deadlines? I had a plan with a schedule, and all of this waiting was putting a damper on it. Sarah also had a plan with a timeline, or so she thought, which is why she decided to move forward with Hagar as her surrogate, regardless of Hagar's thoughts on the matter. Sarah wasn't being patient with God's plan, and neither was I.

For me, patience sometimes feels like pulling hard on the reins of a runaway horse that wants to get to where it's going, and fast. This is a physical feeling felt from within that happens when I need to slow down or put on the brakes in order to be patient with myself or someone else. I've had a lot of practice in recognizing this feeling, so I treat it like a warning signal. Do you have any similar warning signals that go off? If so, practice recognizing these so you can start taking control of your ability to be patient when patience is needed.

Like the horse, I was focused on getting to my goal, which was having another child, and any delay was only getting in my way. But that's not how God works. He wasn't on my timetable, and I needed to be patient with His. So, after reining in my impatient desires and wants, we pivoted and started all over again, back at the beginning.

Being willing to start all over again had its own frustrations. Where do we begin, again? With domestic adoption? Through the foster care system? What is the right road for us to go down? Even though I had an unshakable "knowing" that this was the path God wanted us on, I was not getting any positive feedback. Until we were on vacation, I saw a little plaque in a gift shop with this saying, "Faith is taking the first step even when you can't see the whole staircase."

This was enough for me to rein in my impatience and take *another* first step.

Patience: God's perfect plan is in His timing, not ours

We pivoted from international adoption to domestic adoption. A local adoption agency through Catholic Charities had been in operation for over 100 years. We attended their annual meeting to find out what was involved with domestic adoption, which felt like even more of a long shot than international adoption. The agency supported women who were choosing adoptive families for the child they were carrying.

After pages and pages of paperwork had been completed, a home study conducted, the last step was to create a photobook about your family. The photobooks help each birth mother choose which family she feels best suited to become the adoptive family. It took a while to create this book since we really wanted to give the birth mother a sense of what his or her life would be like as part of our family. Since both my husband and I worked, we introduced her to Miss Peggy's daycare, where our daughter had attended prior to pre-school, and then the pre-school she would attend when old enough. Even our dog, Rearden, made the cut, as well as photos of our home, family, etc.

Finally, the day came in June of 2011, when we were able to hand over a printed book. Upon completion of this last step, we were once again reminded that the average waiting period to hear anything back would be at least 12 to 18 months, if ever, since the agency only placed two or three infants per year. We were told birth mothers associated individuals in our age group to be grandparents rather than adoptive parents, so we were rarely chosen. Therefore, we were encouraged to consider older children who were available for adoption. This is a huge need, but it didn't feel like that was the answer God was pulling me towards. I had honed my mothering skills with my daughter, Katie, who at this point was six years old. Changing diapers, colic, time-out, I was familiar with, but jumping ahead to raising a child experiencing puberty, I was not. In essence, Katie was my little experiment with motherhood. I didn't feel equipped to jump right into mothering an older child.

Do you ever have well-intentioned people strongly suggest a recommendation that you know in your heart of hearts is not the right answer? That was me, respectfully declining their suggestion and mustering my patience to stay with what I felt was God's plan.

My new mantra was "just take the first step" for my breath prayers as I continually looked at my little plaque above the desk. It reminded me to have patience in the process. Once the first step was taken, the rest was in God's hands. I had to be at peace and trust in God with whatever His decision was. We had completed our part.

Now we wait, which is the antithesis of patience. Sarah also waited a long time. She, too, used her age as a marker to cast doubt that she would ever have a child. But then God did a miraculous thing. After seeing Sarah's heartfelt longing for motherhood, He allowed her to overhear a conversation between Him and Abraham. One in which God told Abraham of His plan for Sarah to conceive a son. Abraham found this hard to believe since his response to God was one of skepticism about their being able to conceive, since both he and Sarah were well past their childbearing years. Sarah's disbelief poured through in the laughter to herself (Genesis 18:9-15). Such an unlikely proposition is just as unbelievable thousands of years ago as it is today. But here's the thing: sometimes you've just got to go with it. Whether God tells you literally or figuratively in your heart, you've got to choose to either get out of your own way and let God work His plan or not.

God didn't waste much time with an answer. Two months later, on a hot August afternoon, I received a voicemail at work from our contact at the adoption agency asking me to call her. We had also been told that often documents or other details are missing, so the agency may be contacting us to wrap up any loose ends, which is what I was completely expecting.

Upon my return call, our conversation immediately turned to our book and a birth mother. After a few minutes, it dawned on me, "THIS IS THE CALL!" These were the exact words I used to interrupt the conversation, which were met with a calm response of "Yes, this is the call to let you know your family has been chosen by a birth mother."

Suddenly, a thousand questions flooded my elated mind. The most obvious was, why? Why had the birth mother chosen us? Two reasons stood out, both of which came from our family book. First, she liked knowing we had a plan in place with Miss Peggy for daycare. Second, our dog's name, Rearden, is from the protagonist in *The Atlas Shrugged* by Ayn Rand. This was her favorite book, which created a most meaningful connection.

My husband finally relented to my constant phone calls that kept going to voicemail and excused himself from a board meeting long enough for me to share this incredible news. We were both stunned by how our lives had just changed for the better in an instant. We couldn't wait to tell everyone that our family would be complete by the end of the year. The first person was our daughter, Katie, who had been heavily lobbying for a sister from the beginning, but "You get what you get, and you don't throw a fit." An adage from Miss Peggy, which is still used in our household to this day. Whether a girl or a boy, it didn't matter. I would expect that Sarah felt the same way, but considering God told her she was having a boy, it was a pretty safe bet she knew what to expect.

We were fortunate to meet our birth mother a few months later and then spend more time with her while she was in the hospital. When the day came to bring our baby boy home from the hospital, we were asked what name should be put on the birth certificate. After much deliberation, we decided on Nathaniel, meaning "gift from God".

Upon hearing this, our adoption agency contact, who had asked for the name, had a shocking look on her face. Gathering her composure, she asked if we had spoken with the birth mother that day. No, since we had just gotten to the hospital, we hadn't had time to check in on her yet. Then she explained the reason for her reaction. You see, after every adoptive birth, they ask the birth mother to name the child, for which they are choosing an adoption plan. Nathaniel was the name she had chosen.

With that, all doubt was removed as to whether God's hand had played a role in Nathaniel's birth story. Question marks had been replaced with one rather large period. Patience led to this outcome. God's intended outcome. We had not wasted time considering international adoption or finding the right adoption agency. No, God had simply placed a pause on us. We needed to wait for the right timing, His timing, in order for everything to fall into place and to be as it should.

Hindsight does provide clarity. It confirms that your painstaking patience has paid off. It's from that clarity and learned experience that we take with us to the next situation, when patience may play a crucial role in the outcome of our choices. Wherever you are in your journey with patience, start by taking the first step, then hold onto the reins of that horse when it's just itching to run away, and be patient to see where God leads you. The blessing is in seeing the hand of God at work throughout the whole process once you reach the end.

Start practicing patience on a daily basis with these exercises.

Baby Steps to Becoming More Patient

We have so many opportunities to practice patience throughout our day. Whether it's from tempers flaring in traffic, interrupting someone while they are in the middle of speaking or complaining, either inwardly or overtly, when caught behind another moving much slower than you, as in a checkout line or walkway. All of these examples involve our most precious asset - time. Impatient behavior says, "I'm looking for the fastest way to get to my goal". Patience reins in the out-of-control horse and replaces it with grace.

When choosing to be more patient, the first thing you need to do is realize and acknowledge when you're not. We are all guilty (myself included) of being completely unaware of a behavior we're expressing. Here's a hint: If you're complaining about someone else being impatient, there's a good chance you are too. Ask God to remove the blinders from your eyes and heart so that you can fully see when you find yourself being impatient. Self-awareness is key in changing any behavior.

The next time you find yourself ready to finish another's sentence or story because they are just not getting to the point fast enough—STOP! Don't open your mouth. Don't say a word. As hard as it is to physically restrain yourself, just do it and wait for the other person to finish speaking. Yes, this is easier said than done. I say this from experience since the rude habit of interrupting people is sadly one of my faults. Once you are able to habitually recognize this behavior and react accordingly in little ways, then when the big event comes, which tests your patience, you'll be ready and better able to restrain yourself.

Breathe Prayers

Breathe prayers are short one-sentence prayers that move in rhythm with your breathing, such as "in your timing", "praise you Father God", "your will not mine". This exercise helps to ground you when anxiety is high, often leading to impatience. Not only will your anxious heart rate be slowed, but your focus will be redirected to God rather than the issue at hand.

Chapter 3

Grace Tested: Dealing with Difficult People

By Marilynn Lester

AS A PRISONER FOR THE LORD, THEN, I URGE YOU TO LIVE A LIFE WORTHY OF THE CALLING YOU HAVE RECEIVED. BE COMPLETELY HUMBLE AND GENTLE; BE PATIENT, BEARING WITH ONE ANOTHER IN LOVE. MAKE EVERY EFFORT TO KEEP THE UNITY OF THE SPIRIT THROUGH THE BOND OF PEACE.

EPHESIANS 4:1-3

There was a time when our son was in and out of courts with probation stacked upon probation. Finally, the judge said, "I sentence you to 180 days." The sound of his gavel echoed through the courtroom, and that was that. The judge rose and left, and I stood in stunned silence. A rock settled in the pit of my stomach. I calculated in my mind what 180 days were, "That's six months!" I groaned inwardly. All the praying and Christian teaching we had instilled in this son seemed to have evaporated into thin air. "How long, O Lord? Will he ever learn?"

At the same time, I was teaching music in one of the most challenging schools in our city. The stress was incredible. Teachers in this school encountered difficult students, challenging parents, and an administration requiring them to deliver expert education that brought results from children who did not want to learn--always maintaining professionalism with a smile on their faces.

There seemed to be one challenge piled upon another in my life at that time. Would there be no end?

A few years later, in a pre-school, I counted...

"17, 18, 19.... Boys (inward gasp) oh my!"

"1, 2, 3...?3...?3...? - aren't there any more girls? (inward groan) Oh my!"

No wonder the classroom seemed to be in constant motion with the din raised to an unbelievable decibel level. Now, in a church-based preschool situation, this was the beginning of a very eventful school year with nineteen four-year-old boys and three four-year-old girls in one class. I'm not a sexist, but there are definite differences between boys and girls even at this tender age. Boys tend to be louder, more active, and more aggressive. I said, "tend to be". There are girls who can match and even surpass boys in this, but when you get nineteen four-year-old boys together in one place, you have the recipe for trouble. I needed help.

That was the year I finally started learning what it meant to be filled with the Spirit. I knew the characteristics of the Spirit-filled life. I could recite them off the top of my head. "But the fruit of the Spirit is love, joy, peace, patience, kindness, goodness, faithfulness, gentleness and self-control...." (Galatians 5:22,23, ESV). But that year, I began to experience them in my own life when the Lord taught me what it means to be filled with the Spirit. I prayed every morning for this filling. It was only through the power of the Holy Spirit that I made it through that year.

Relinquishing control of my life to the Holy Spirit gave me new boldness and peace, new freedom and confidence. I experienced patience that I knew did not come from me. There still was the chaos, but I had strength in my heart that enabled me to handle things as they came.

I wish I had known that secret when I was facing the judge with our son. I wish I had known that secret when I was teaching in those difficult schools in the city. I finally learned it when teaching preschoolers. It was then that I began to experience the power of the Holy Spirit. Through these children, I experienced the strength God gives. Parents and teachers have the dubious task of trying to mold clay that is constantly moving. I heard it said one time, "Teaching preschoolers was like trying to herd cats." By myself, it is impossible; but through the Holy Spirit, I have victory.

Difficult relationships can occur at home with family members, at school with students and teachers, and at work with bosses and co-workers. Even in ministries at church, thorny situations make it difficult to minister side by side. Anywhere people are trying to live and work for the Lord, Satan wants to stir up discord. Wherever parents and teachers are trying to train children to follow the Lord, Satan works doubly hard to turn hearts away. We all become impatient and wonder, "How long, O Lord?"

But Jesus prayed for us before He went to the cross. He petitioned the Father more than once in that single prayer, "that they may be one as We are one" (John 17:11, 21, 22, 23). Jesus knew that by the unity of believers that the world would know we are his disciples. He puts us in the most demanding situations where there is no way we could possibly achieve unity in our own power. Only in the power of the Holy Spirit can we live in harmony, and all the glory goes to him.

Walking in the flesh

> "I urge you to live a life worthy of the calling
> you have received..." Ephesians 4:1b

When we walk in the flesh, a plethora of negative characteristics come to the surface. Paul points out to the Galatians that our flesh wars against the Spirit and the Spirit against the flesh. A constant battle wages within ourselves. The works of the flesh are "sexual immorality, impurity and debauchery; idolatry and witchcraft; hatred, discord, jealousy, fits of rage, selfish ambition, dissensions, factions and envy; drunkenness, orgies, and the like" (Galatians 5:19-21a).

Many of these fleshly works relate to our relationships with other people: "hatred, discord, jealousy, fits of rage, selfish ambition, dissensions, factions and envy..." (Galatians 5:20). These things should not characterize the Christian, but they happen when we allow our natural nature to have control. These characteristics are not part of "a life worthy of the calling".

Examples in the Bible abound with people controlled by the flesh. Jealousy caused Cain to take his brother's life. Self-gratification caused Esau to sell his birthright to Jacob, which led to a rivalry that still exists to this day. Even Moses, when the children of Israel constantly complained, struck the rock in a fit of rage instead of speaking to it, which cost him the opportunity to enter Canaan with the rest of Israel.

The call to wait

Those who want to live by the Spirit are called on to "Commit your way to the Lord; trust in Him, and He will act" (Psalm 37:5, ESV). David repeatedly wrote about when the wicked prosper, and we are struggling, what are we supposed to do? David encouraged us to resort to praise as we remember what the Lord had done in the past and have faith in what God is able to do in the future.

At one point, David in the Psalms said, "Be still before the Lord and wait patiently for him; do not fret when people succeed in their ways, when they carry out their wicked schemes... A little while, and the wicked will be no more; though you look for them, they will not be found. But the meek will inherit the land and enjoy great peace." (Psalm 37:7,10,11) Don't worry. God sees your turmoil and cares. With patience and trust, we can wait for the time when we will inherit the land and enjoy peace and success.

It's hard to see people who have offended us succeed. Waiting is a challenge for parents who see other children excelling in school and sports, while they know their own children are struggling in these areas, but are excelling in Christian principles. An even heavier burden comes if their children are not living for the Lord when they have poured so much time and effort into their spiritual training. At such a time, we must remember discouragement is always from

Satan. In the meantime, God wants us to be still as we wait patiently to see the results of God working in our child's life. This patience is made possible through the power of the Holy Spirit.

Walking by the Spirit

A person whose life is "worthy of the calling you have received" shows signs of being humble and gentle, being patient, bearing with one another in love (Ephesians 4:1-3). Compare this description with the description of a person who is filled with the Spirit in Paul's letter to the Galatians. The Spirit will be producing fruit of "love, joy, peace, patience, kindness, goodness, faithfulness, gentleness, self-control..." (Galatians 5:22-23). How can we do all that when everything and everyone is against us?

Being filled with the Holy Spirit is not automatic like the indwelling of the Spirit at salvation. Being filled depends on our willingness to yield to the Holy Spirit and allow Him control in our lives. We are commanded to be filled with the Spirit, and, when we commit ourselves to the Spirit and ask him, he fills us.

Every believer is at a different point in their walk with Christ, and, therefore, the extent to which we allow control of the Holy Spirit will be different in every Christian. When we ask, He honors our request and causes a change in our character.

It is important to note: the request and the filling of the Spirit are repeated events. It must be done repeatedly, as our natural desires tend to take over. Our flesh is still warring against our Spirit. When I was teaching that class of preschoolers, I prayed every day for the filling of the Spirit. If I didn't, my flesh would easily take over. There were times when I did fall flat on my face. There were times when I expected maturity from those children, which they did not have. In those times, I contritely asked for forgiveness and the filling again. God, in His grace, picked me up, brushed me off, and sent me out to meet my challenges again with the Holy Spirit's power within me.

The filling of the Holy Spirit is not obtained by self-effort. We can only claim victory by allowing the Holy Spirit to live through us. When I was teaching those nineteen boys, I could relax and allow the Holy Spirit to love and be patient through me. If I tried my hardest to love them, I would fall flat on my face. Knowing all the characteristics of the fruit of the Spirit by heart is not enough. I started experiencing those characteristics in my life by yielding.

The Bible instructs us, "Do not get drunk with wine, for that is debauchery, but be filled with the Spirit" (Ephesians 5:18, ESV). The more we allow the Holy Spirit to be in our lives, the less room there will be for ourselves. We yield our rights to the control of the Holy Spirit instead of demanding our rights in the flesh. You will know that the Holy Spirit is in control by the peace that floods your soul.

When I knew the Holy Spirit was in control, I was able to relax and enjoy all the little boys' differences, their excitement, and their creativity. Creativity is just another way of saying differences that go against the status quo and standard rules and regulations. These are things that could really irk a person who is expecting a neat and orderly classroom.

Paul tells the Thessalonians, "Do not quench the Spirit." (1 Thessalonians 5:19). We quench the Spirit by not listening to him. John F. Walvoord, in his book *The Holy Spirit,* states, "It is evident that refusal to submit to the Word of God is quenching the Spirit, making the fullness of the Spirit impossible."[1] When we refuse to obey the simplest commands of God in His Word, when we love the world more than God, or when we let the noise of the world drown out the voice of God, we cannot hear the Holy Spirit, and we quench the power of the Spirit.

The Holy Spirit will at times speak to us in a still small voice, which you know is the voice of the Spirit. Sometimes the Holy Spirit speaks to us through written words on the page, in black and white. In the New Testament, there are many instructions regarding our relationship with other people. It would be overwhelming to even consider following all these instructions except through the power of the Holy Spirit.

Jesus instructed his disciples that the greatest commandment of all time is, "Love the Lord your God with all your heart, with all your soul, and with all your mind." (Matthew 22:37). He continued by saying, "And the second is like it, 'Love your neighbor as yourself.'" (Matthew 22:39).

Some of the other guidelines relating to our relationships are:

> "Be devoted to one another in love. Honor one another above yourselves" (Romans 12:10).

> "Be kind and compassionate to one another, forgiving each other, just as in Christ God forgave you" (Ephesians 4:32).

"Therefore encourage one another and build each other up…" (1 Thessalonians 5:11).

"Let us not become conceited, provoking and envying each other" (Galatians 5:26).

"And let us consider how we may spur one another on toward love and good deeds, not giving up meeting together, as some are in the habit of doing, but encouraging one another—and all the more as you see the Day approaching" (Hebrews 10:24-25).

God knows we need each other as we battle against the Evil One. We need encouragement through love shown by good deeds and fellowship. Strength against the enemy is bolstered when we build each other up, and God's name is honored when there is unity in the Christian community.

I had the opportunity to present a devotional to a group of faculty members at a Christian college shortly after I began to experience the filling of the Spirit in this way. I began by saying, "I've quit trying to love other people…" I could see the college president out of the corner of my eye with his head down, his hands over his eyes, and shaking his head.

But I went on to say, "I quit trying to love other people in my own power. If we experience the filling of the Holy Spirit, loving others comes with the package. If we are filled with the Holy Spirit, the characteristics of His fruit will be overflowing in our lives."

Benefits of Patience

By applying the filling of the Holy Spirit to our lives, we continually become more like Jesus Christ. This is called "progressive sanctification". We don't attain perfection all at once but are changed through time. Paul wrote to the Corinthians, "And we all, with unveiled faces contemplate the Lord's glory, are being transformed into his image with ever-increasing glory, which comes from the Lord, who is the Spirit" (2 Corinthians 3:18). We could describe the glory of the Lord with words similar to the characteristics of the fruit of the Spirit. The glory of the Lord is seen in our faces when we yield to the Spirit, and it is felt in our relationships.

John Walvoord said, "... progressive sanctification does not proceed from self-effort or from the will of the natural man, nor does it proceed from the new nature itself. It is a product of the Holy Spirit wrought in a yielded life. The all-important fact is that true Christian character cannot be produced apart from the Holy Spirit."[1]

James, the brother of Jesus, the author of the book of James, encourages the Israelites who were dispersed to continue in their faith even though they were encountering trials in this world. He says, "Consider it pure joy, my brothers and sisters, whenever you face trials of many kinds, because you know that the testing of your faith produces perseverance. Let perseverance finish its work so that you may be mature and complete, not lacking anything." (James 1:2-4, NKJV).

When we endure our challenging relationships in a God-honoring way, we will be moving toward maturity as a child of God. Age doesn't necessarily bring maturity; testing does... when we allow the Holy Spirit to do His work.

We are on a journey

We are on a journey from our natural human selves to becoming more like Jesus Christ. All believers are on this same journey. We are all at different points along the way. Therefore, when we pray for those who challenge us, have patience waiting on God to work in that person's life.

We have patience because we have faith in the work of God. "Now faith is confidence in what we hope for and assurance about what we do not see" (Hebrews 11:1). When we pray, we don't see what's on the other side of that prayer. We don't see God working, but we trust that He is. Our call is to pray for those who have offended us and trust that God is working. We then wait with patience until the change is evident.

Sometimes that change doesn't come for a long time. Sometimes that change happens in our own lives instead, as we become more like Christ. Even the heroes of faith did not see the promises fulfilled, but they continued to have faith.

A number of years ago, I experienced a hurtful situation while serving in ministry at church. I was crushed. I could not face that person for a long time without resentment and hurt. He eventually moved away, but I knew I still had to learn to forgive. Since then, I've learned a lot about forgiveness and how to express it.

When we forgive, we are not saying that what that person did was ok. We are just saying we accept that person as a brother or sister in Christ, and by the grace of God, we will let go of the hurt for the bond of peace. Some situations do need to be dealt with face-to-face in the attitude of love.

Sometimes we just need to learn to deal with it in our own hearts.

Recently, that person returned to the area for a visit. I prayed, asking God to give me grace if I had to meet him face to face. At that time, the word "grace" was revealed to me in a fresh and new way. It became one more word to add to my vocabulary for forgiveness. Grace is something we receive which we do not deserve, as the forgiveness God offers to us, even while we were yet sinners. We extend grace to the offender as God extends grace to us. It turned out that I did not have to face that person, but I felt peace flooding my soul. I knew in my heart the relationship was beginning to heal because I was offering grace on my journey to forgiveness.

As we are waiting for God to change someone, hopefully, we are learning to forgive that person. Paul exhorts us to "Be kind and compassionate to one another, forgiving each other, just as in Christ God forgave you." (Ephesians 4:32). Since God forgave us even while we were still sinners, God expects us to forgive others even before they ask for forgiveness or show any signs of changing or even admitting they may have done something wrong.

The Bible says, "Walk by the Spirit, and you will not gratify the desires of the flesh" (Galatians 5:16, ESV). Paul exhorts the Ephesian church to not follow their fleshly desires, but "be filled with the Spirit" (Ephesians 5:18b, ESV). Eventually, this filling will result in being able to worship side by side, "speaking to one another with psalms and hymns and spiritual songs, singing and making melody to the Lord with your heart." (Ephesians 5:19, ESV).

***

The year my son was sentenced to 180 days in jail, he was released and home by Christmas. For Christmas, he gave me a little cherub figurine. These little cherubs, in many ways, represent different scenarios of life. The one he gave me was wearing a policeman's cap, and it had the year stamped on the bottom. He said he didn't want me to forget that year – as if I ever would. I kept it around just to remind me of the relationship my son and I have, and remind me of my son's weird sense of humor. Just recently, I picked it up, and a leg broke off, yet I still keep it displayed on my desk with that broken leg. That break reminds me that he has broken away from his past. I mentioned this to him, and he totally agreed. That past is gone. He is now living a new life.

He's not perfect yet, but neither am I. It was while I was waiting for God to change others that He changed me. None of us reaches perfection until we reach the heavenly shores. We must keep praying as we patiently trust the Lord to change us and others.

We don't pray for patience. We pray for the filling of the Holy Spirit. As we yield to him and allow Him to have control, we experience the patience that can only come from the Spirit, and we give glory to God. When we pray, we don't know what's going on in the other person's heart and mind. We must trust God to be working his best in each life. We may not see it right away, but if we are patient, he will bring it to pass in his own timing and in his own way.

When dealing with difficult people, Paul tells the believers in Rome, "If it is possible, as far as it depends on you, live at peace with everyone" (Romans 12:18). Later in this same letter, Paul encourages the Roman believers, "We who are strong have an obligation to bear with the failings of the weak, and not to please ourselves" (Romans 15:1, ESV). It doesn't matter where they are on their journey; we must make our best effort to live at peace with all people.

In His Sermon on the Mount, Jesus said, "Love your enemies, and pray for those who persecute you..." (Matthew 5:44, ESV). Love is defined by Paul in his letter to the Corinthians. "Love is patient, love is kind, it is not jealous; love does not brag, it is not arrogant. It does not act disgracefully, it does not see its own benefit; it is not provoked, does not keep an account of a wrong suffered, it does not rejoice in unrighteousness, but rejoices with the truth; it keeps every confidence, it believes all things, hopes all things, endures all things" (1 Corinthians 13:4-7, ESV). Love requires an overabundance of patience obtained only from the Holy Spirit.

Our responsibility is to live at peace with everyone, pray for those who have offended us, forgive in love, and be patient waiting for the answers to our prayers. But, even before our prayers are answered, we extend grace as God extended grace to us while we were still sinners. We are all at a different point on our journey. We are all in need of God's grace.

As I concluded writing this chapter, I was confronted with another opportunity to practice what I've been preaching. It's not easy when the wound is fresh. What do you do or how should you feel when a ministry you poured a lot of your best time and effort into is faced with extinction at the hands of other people? I had to go back and reread what I wrote, allowing the Holy Spirit to speak to me through the Word of God. I had to pray for the filling of the Holy Spirit and for his power to overcome feelings of rejection, despair, and defeat. Now, I must patiently wait for God's work in my life and in the lives of others.

Action

- Pray for those who have hurt you or caused distress in your life.
- Forgive them.
- Love in obedience to Christ's command.
- Have faith that God is working in their lives as well as yours.
- Watch for a change in your own life.

Chapter 4

Divinely Orchestrated Love:
It's Worth the Wait

By Lisa Recor

LOVE IS PATIENT, LOVE IS KIND. IT DOES NOT ENVY, IT DOES NOT BOAST, IT IS NOT PROUD...LOVE DOES NOT DELIGHT IN EVIL BUT REJOICES WITH THE TRUTH. IT ALWAYS PROTECTS, ALWAYS TRUSTS, ALWAYS HOPES, ALWAYS PERSEVERES.
−1 CORINTHIANS 13:4,6-7

When I pulled out onto the interstate, I was passed by a Black Ford F-150 with a German Shepherd in the rear seat. I thought I was seeing things! I'd had a dream that morning that I would see Jack and meet him on the highway. When I saw him, my heart leaped in my chest! I knew that God had heard my prayers and was bringing him back to me. That month that Jack was gone seemed like a lifetime while I waited patiently for God to work.

How It All Began

Jack and I met in October of 2012 at a small bar in Northern New York. I was there with a friend. It wasn't a place that I normally hung out at, and this handsome guy walked in with bright blue eyes, a big smile, a swagger, and a shiny bald head. I was immediately smitten. Our eyes kept connecting. He finally walked up and asked me to dance. The band was playing "Tiny Dancer", a cover by Elton John. Oh, he was smooth on the dance floor, and he smelled amazing.

Jack was a widower. His wife died in June that year. They served the Lord faithfully together for twenty years. When Melody died, Jack backslid. He was mad at God because he was believing for Mel's healing to take place here on earth. She got her ultimate healing, just not the way they expected. So after twenty years, Jack returned to the bar scene, drinking again after years of abstinence. He was trying to fill the God-sized void in his heart.

I had recently divorced....again. I didn't have a relationship with God, but He was instrumental in helping me get out of a bad situation and settle into a place for my 11-year-old daughter and me that was exactly what I could afford. I was deeply immersed in New Age beliefs, and God was drawing me into Himself. I had begun listening to Christian music in September, just before I met Jack. This change in music affected both my daughter and me. I felt God drawing us to Him.

Jack and I kept running into each other and eventually exchanged phone numbers. We started seeing more of each other and grew closer over the coming months, to each other and to the Lord. As much as Jack didn't want to serve God because he was still mad, He used Jack to bring me into a relationship with Him. Jack shared with me how God was speaking to him and using him to testify and help others. This built my faith. I wanted that kind of relationship with

God. I wanted to hear His voice and have Him use me to encourage others.

My First Experience With Patience

Jack and I are both big Syracuse Orange men's basketball fans, and at the end of March 2013, the team was vying for a trip to the Sweet 16. I had called and asked Jack to come over for dinner and watch the game. He said he wasn't feeling well and thought he should stay home. Do you ever have those inklings? Those feelings that just kind of nag at you? I told him that I felt he shouldn't be alone. He finally agreed. It was a good thing too! The game went late that night. I went to bed before it ended. I woke up to Jack yelling for me. When I came downstairs, he was gray and had broken out in a cold sweat. He thought it was heartburn and sent me to get his Tums, then he was going home. I'm like, "You're not going anywhere but the hospital!" He is so stubborn! He wanted to drive himself! I couldn't get him to allow me to call 9-1-1, but he finally agreed to let me drive him to the hospital, which was about 20 minutes away.

We got there just in time! He was having a massive heart attack! His right coronary artery was 100% blocked! While Jack had a heart catheterization performed and a stent placed in his blocked artery, I sat in the waiting room. At first, I was pacing, impatient, even fearful, wanting to know what was going on. I think it was the first time I remember praying. I didn't know if God would listen, but I felt reassured that Jack was in God's very capable hands. I truly entrusted Jack to God. As I did, there was a sense of peace that washed over me. It was definitely a peace that surpassed all understanding (Philippians 4:7).

I'd never felt like that before. In that moment, I knew that prayer turned my impatience into patience. It shifted my focus. It took away my fear. It eliminated my desire to control the situation. I was able to surrender everything to the One in full control, and it calmed my own heart. I shudder to think, even to this day, what would have happened if Jack hadn't come over that night. I know what would have happened. He wouldn't be here today. God was in the middle of all of that!

The Trip That Changed My Life

In mid-September, Jack decided to take a trip to Kentucky to look for hunting land. I asked if he wanted company. He did, so I went along. We spent a week in Southern Kentucky touring the countryside and looking at different properties. I felt very drawn here. There was an overwhelming pull. I told Jack on the way back to New York that I wanted to spend the rest of my life in Kentucky. He thought I was a bit nuts and was concerned about what I'd do and where I'd live. God took care of that, too!

Two weeks later, I was back in Kentucky interviewing for a job. I was hired on the spot, and my then 12-year-old daughter and I moved two days after Christmas. The company that hired me connected me with a realtor, and I rented a 3-bedroom house in Bowling Green, KY, sight unseen. I still did not have a relationship with Jesus...yet... But he was orchestrating my every move. Literally.

Long Distance Love Builds Patience

Jack was not ready to move. He was not ready to commit to me fully, so we did the long-distance thing. He'd come down and stay for a month or two and go back to New York for a month or two. I'd go to New York for a long week-end or just a week when I could take a vacation. This went on for over two years. Long-distance relationships require commitment, trust, love, mutual support, and an incredible amount of patience. I was always waiting for Jack. I waited for his phone calls. I waited for him to visit. I waited for him to come to his senses. Psalm 27:14 (NLT) says, "Wait patiently for the Lord. Be brave and be courageous. Wait patiently for the Lord." So I did! God kept reassuring me that Jack was the one. When Jack visited, we went to church. God used Jack through all of this to help me in my walk. If I had questions, Jack would get his bible out and show me in the Word where my answers were. I started to see Jack through God's eyes. I began to see everything through God's eyes.

The Test and Trial

In December of 2015, I bought a house in Franklin, KY. Jack came down and helped us pack and move. At this point, I'd been in Kentucky for two years and had come to the saving knowledge of Jesus Christ. I answered the call that I felt on my first visit. It was time to walk out the rest of my life with Jesus. There was no specific date when I fell to my knees. I had been on a journey and decided to commit to serving the Lord with my whole heart. When that happened, things got a little complicated for Jack and me. The Holy Spirit was convicting me and changing me. He was making me into a new creation. When that happened, I realized that I was living in sin. I was very much like the Samaritan woman at the well (John 4). I had been married four times, and I was sharing a bed with a man who was not my husband.

My very best friend lived in Texas outside of Dallas. She had invited me to visit and celebrate her 50th birthday. This was June of 2016. At first, I was going to take Jack, but I decided against it. Things between us were tense, and we ultimately broke it off just before I left for Texas.

Saying goodbye to Jack after being together for three and a half years just broke my heart. I was being convicted to walk this new life with Jesus, and Jack was still stuck in the past, not ready to let go of it and the world that had crept back in. He was not ready to commit to me. I just couldn't continue to live in sin, without God in the center of our lives, and without a full commitment from Jack. I wanted more. I deserved more.

When I came back from Texas that first week of June, I went through everything that was Jack: pictures, poems, cards, and a scrapbook that I had made for him. I blocked him from my phone and my daughter's. I burned pictures of him, thinking that if I didn't see him, I wouldn't miss him, but I missed him terribly. As I looked back at poems I'd written, I realized that God was showing me something profound. I realized that I had always seen Jack through God's eyes. There was so much more to him that even he would never see in himself.

Praying Patiently Through the Wait

Ephesians 4:2 (NLT) says, "Always be humble and gentle. Be patient with each other, making allowance for each other's faults because of your love." I knew that if we were really meant to be together, God would work it out. I just knew that God had big plans to restore Jack and that there was a prominent place for me in his life. I began to pray, "Lord, if there's a will and a way, that You want us back together, I leave it all in Your very capable hands to do exceedingly and abundantly above, immeasurably more than I could ever ask, think, dream, or imagine (Ephesians 3:20). Jack always said we are better together than we are apart. He was Yours first, Lord. Have Your way in him and in our relationship. In Jesus' name."

So I waited, patiently trusting the God of the Universe to make a way where there seemed to be no way. Practical patience allows others the grace to grow and change. It allows us to grow and change as well. I was being changed. As my faith grew, so did my patience. 2 Peter 1:5-7 says:

> For this very reason, make every effort to add to your faith goodness; and to goodness, knowledge; and to knowledge, self-control; and to self-control, perseverance; and to perseverance, godliness; and to godliness, mutual affection; and to mutual affection, love.

I believe that being apart tested the level of our commitment. We had built a solid foundation. We had some things to work out, but only God knew what was going on with each of us.

A Divine Appointment

I returned to New York the following month to spend the 4th of July weekend with my oldest daughter and her husband. On my last day there, which fell on the 4th, we decided to go golfing. I went to get my golf clubs out of my car, and I found it had a flat tire. On a holiday! What was I going to do? The only thing I could do was to take it to the Walmart service center. There was no one else open, and I couldn't wait. I had to leave the next day because of work. So I dropped my car off at Walmart, and they fixed the tire while I went golfing. When I came back to pick it up, they told me I had to drive it 50 miles the next day to another Walmart to make sure the plug they put in the tire would hold.

I found a Walmart in Geneva, NY, just off Interstate 90 and just 50 miles from my daughter's house. I worked out the timing of my departure so that I would arrive at the service center as it opened. When I left, I told my daughter that I'd had a dream that morning, just before I awoke, that I was going to meet Jack on the highway. She was like, "No way, Mom! That will never happen!"

I pulled into that Walmart in Geneva just as they were opening the overhead doors. A technician was nice enough to come out and check my tire, and he gave me the go-ahead to travel back to Kentucky. I wasn't out on the road for 10 minutes when this Black Ford F-150 with a German Shepherd in the rear seat zipped by me. I was like, "Are you kidding me right now, God?" I pulled out into the left lane and sped up a bit to catch up with it. As soon as I got behind it, I recognized the license plate. It WAS Jack! I took a picture and sent it to my daughter. Her return text said, "No way!" Yes way! Now what?

We played this game of cat and mouse on the highway. Jack would be driving in the right lane. I'd pass him on the left, then pull in front of him. He would pull out to pass me on the left and get back in front of me in the right lane. We did this little passing game for miles and miles. All the while, he had no idea it was me. Then, this one time, just before we hit Buffalo, it finally hit him. He passed me and looked over with his arms up. He had this amazed look of "What the heck?"

So I picked up my phone, unblocked him, and called. Jack answered. We were both stunned, in shock, actually. We decided to pull off at the next rest area and meet. When we got out of our vehicles, the first words Jack exclaimed were, "What are the chances?" I said, "It had to be God! There's no other way!"

I found out he was indeed headed to Kentucky. He was going to stay with a mutual friend of ours in Bowling Green. While visiting, he had set up an appointment with a realtor to look at a house. We shared how much we'd missed each other. I told him that if he was up for it, he could stay with us, but he had to sleep on the couch. He agreed. We had a lot to discuss, and that would give us a chance to catch up, seek the Lord, and figure out what was next.

Answered Prayer

During our time of separation, Jack had realized that he missed me, that he was ready to put his property in New York on the market, and that he wanted a future with me. He realized that what he always said was true: "We really are stronger together than we are apart!" It took a year for his property to sell. When Jack moved in with my daughter and me in Franklin, he was still not ready for a piece of paper to say that we were married. He was ready, however, to commit to me and make a life with me, so I ordered rings for us to exchange. We stood in our kitchen, with my daughter as a witness, and before God we committed our lives to each other.

I was confident that we had taken a step in the right direction. I felt that God honored our commitment, and I knew He would work out the rest. Ecclesiastes 4:12 says, "Though one may be overpowered, two can defend themselves. A cord of three strands is not quickly broken." God has been at the center of our relationship from day one. He has brought us together to strengthen us, to encourage each other, to pray for each other, and to grow as one flesh. We purchased a 60-acre farm with a one-bedroom barndominium in August of 2021. The following January, we decided to build a house because we had no room for company. Within days of that decision, God answered that prayer that I had been patiently waiting on for years.

The Proposal

Jack had written my first name with his last name on a piece of paper and put it in front of me. I pushed it back and said, "Whatever." He pushed it back and said, "I think it has a nice ring to it, don't you?" I said, "It does, but you've said that'll never happen." He said, "I think it's time. Will you marry me?"

Well, it doesn't take a genius to figure out that my answer was a very excited and resounding, "Yes!" We were married on the porch of our new home, which we were building together, on June 25th, 2022. Our Pastor officiated. We were joined by his wife, my youngest daughter and her husband, and my best friend and her husband. My oldest daughter and my mom tuned in via FaceTime. It was a sweet ceremony and oh so special. It was truly an answered prayer and a dream come true.

Takeaways

There's an adage credited to Richard Bach that says, "If you love something, set it free; if it comes back, it's yours; if it doesn't, it never was." I found out just how much truth there is in this quote. I also found the importance of standing on God's promises. After God made Adam from the dust, He realized that His otherwise excellent creation needed a helpmate, so He created Eve out of Adam's rib. She was Adam's perfect complement. Man cannot fulfill his created purpose alone.

· Let Go & Let God

At some point, faith requires release. Sometimes we have to let go and let God. There's a time and a purpose for everything under heaven. There's a time to search and a time to quit searching (Ecclesiastes 3:1,6). We have to have faith in God. He has the perfect spouse picked out for each of us. You will find that person in God's timing, or in my case, He will bring back the right one for you in His timing. God's timing is always perfect, and His plans are always perfect.

When Jack and I broke up after my return from Texas, I had to let go and let God. I had to surrender what I wanted. I knew God would do with Jack exactly what was needed. He would bring Jack to the place where He needed him. I was holding on to God's promises of a helpmate. I was holding on to what I saw in Jack through God's eyes. I loved Jack so much that I knew that if I truly let him go with no contact, no interference on my part, God would bring him back to me if we were truly meant to be. I let go, surrendered Jack to God, and let God do what only He can do.

· Trust God

Trust is built in the waiting. Trust God that He has a plan and a purpose for your life, that includes your spouse. "And we know that in all things God works for the good of those who love Him, who have been called according to His purpose" (Romans 8:28). This has been a go-to verse for me to lean on, for all kinds of reasons, and it remains strong and true. Sometimes, just when things seem to fall apart, God steps in and brings it all back together. Sometimes, He makes it better than we could have asked. He builds back better.

"The Lord is good to those who wait for him, to the soul who seeks him" (Lamentations 3:25, ESV). I sought the Lord, and I waited, and look what He did! I never would have anticipated the life that we have. I was happy living in our little country house in Franklin, but God had something even better in store for us. We have since been called to ministry together. Jack has a heart for the lost, and I have a heart to disciple them. We didn't know what God was doing with us when we went through that separation; we just knew that He had a purpose for us, and we trusted that He'd make it known, and He did. Don't rush the process.

What God is building in the waiting is just as important as what you're waiting for.

Believe God & His Word

What you believe shapes how you wait. Believe that God is the God of more, that He can do more than you could ever dream. Ephesians 3:20 is my life verse. The NKJV translation says, "Now to Him who is able to do exceedingly abundantly above all that we ask or think, according to the power that works in us." We had a Pastor years ago who encouraged us to "dare-ask" God for big things, things that only He can do, things that cannot be done by humans, in human strength, or with human influence. He's a big God, and sometimes we put Him in little boxes. God is limitless. He's all-knowing, all-seeing, and He's everywhere all at once.

I was so much like the woman at the well, and at one time, I was struggling and ashamed. I didn't believe that I could be loved by anyone, let alone God. BUT GOD! He knew my heart. Not only did He show me that I was worthy to be loved by Him, but God brought me Jack. God brought me a man who not only loves me, but he's also been instrumental in helping me grow in my faith. Jack helped me in so many ways to understand that God and Jesus are One. I was so entrenched in a New Age mindset when we met in that hole-in-the-wall bar in the middle of Northern New York. While we were both lost and broken, God intervened. God knew we needed each other. He had a plan and a purpose for our lives that we couldn't have known back then. God helped us grow together. Don't shrink your expectations to match your situation. Let your faith rise to match who God is.

Encouragement

Waiting is not wasted time. It's preparation. While I was patiently waiting for God to intervene, He was at work behind the scenes the whole time. He was building my faith so that I could stand steadfast in it. God was moving. Jack didn't know that I was in New York that 4th of July. I didn't know that Jack was headed back to Kentucky because he'd had a change of heart. Jack didn't know about my dream of meeting him on the highway. Only God knew all of the pieces to the puzzle. He masterfully orchestrated an intricate plan, one that only He could devise. One where Jack and I both left New York at virtually the same time, both headed to Kentucky, to meet on a highway in Western New York at just the right moment. It was definitely a kairos time. God manifested. God created. God timed!

Love IS patient. Love IS kind. Love ALWAYS trusts, ALWAYS hopes, and ALWAYS perseveres (1 Corinthians 13:4,7). I knew that Jack was the man for me! God had brought us through too much for too long. I HAD to trust Him, to have faith in Him, to believe in Him, to be oh so patient with Him as He worked out everything right down to the smallest detail. I had to be patient with Jack through this process and patient with God while He worked on Him. Don't get me wrong, God was working on me, too.

I encourage you to be patient in the process as well. Psalm 37:4 (ESV) says, "Delight yourself in the LORD, and he will give you the desires of your heart." Seek Him. God knows! The more time you spend with God, the more your desires align. Have faith that He has the perfect spouse picked out for you. Trust Him that He will make that known to you because His plans and purposes for you are good, and He works all things for good for those who love Him. Believe that He can do the impossible. Believe that He can do immeasurably more, exceeding your every hope, your every dream, your every prayer. Be still and know that He is God. (Psalm 46:10)

"Wait patiently for the Lord. Be brave and courageous. Yes, wait patiently for the Lord" (Psalm 27:14, NLT). God promises in Jeremiah 29:11 that His plans for you are good, to give you a future and a hope. He designed and created us to be in a relationship with Him and to have a helpmate to walk it out. Stand on this promise from Ecclesiastes and wait patiently for the Lord to answer:

> Two are better than one, because they have a good return for their labor. If either of them falls down, one can help the other up. If two people lie together, they will keep warm. Though one may be overpowered, two can defend themselves. A cord of three strands is not quickly broken.
>
> Ecclesiastes 4:9-12

Next Steps

- Seek the Lord and serve Him. Make time to spend with God every day. Stay faithful in the waiting. Stay anchored in His Word. Stay expectant. Get in the secret place where you can share the desires of your heart and where you can grow to trust Him.

- Be expectant and don't settle. God will never lead you astray. You have been made for more. He will always be with you, even while you wait patiently for the one He's chosen for you. Jesus said in Mark 11:24 (NLT), "I tell you, you can pray for anything, and if you believe that you've received it, it will be yours." So believe!

- Pray. Devote yourself to prayer and allow the Lord to do the rest. Pray for your future husband:

Heavenly Father, I lift my future husband to You. Protect him and keep him safe. Draw him closer to You every day. I pray for him to have a righteous heart, a spirit of humility, wisdom, and the courage to lead well. I pray that he is surrounded by godly influence and friends who hold him accountable. Prepare him to be a godly husband and the spiritual leader of our home. Work on my own heart, Lord, to be the woman you want me to be. Help me to be a Proverbs 31 woman who is virtuous and righteous, who is clothed in strength and dignity, who laughs without fear of the future. I trust that You have the perfect man picked out for me, a man after Your own heart, who loves You, puts You first, who prays and spends time with You daily, and who wants to serve You in all ways. I trust you, Lord, for Your wisdom, for Your lovingkindness, for Your grace, and for Your perfect timing. When my future spouse crosses my path, may I know that I know that I know that this man is the one You've picked out just for me. I ask all this in Jesus' name. Amen and amen!

Chapter 5

Patience Came Through the Calm

By Kathleen Fischer

I was an excellent swimmer and decided to do a surface dive into the lake. As I dove into the lake, the dock moved, and I hit the sandy lake bottom. In that split second, I knew I had broken my neck and swam to the surface. I began yelling toward my fiancé, David, who was standing on the dock. I could not feel my legs, but I was determined to doggy paddle to the dock. At this time, no one had cell phones to call emergency services. On this particular day, David flagged my parents down as they arrived at the campground. They parked their car in the grassy area. I had my fiancé pull me onto the dock and carry me to their car. He laid me flat in the back seat. My parents drove me to the nearest hospital, and David followed us in his car.

There was no trauma center, so I was placed in an ambulance for transport to South Bend Memorial Hospital. The county hospital staff put me in a hospital gown with a straight jacket so I could not move, around my head sandbags, and strapped me to the gurney for stability. I arrived at the trauma center, and the following week was a blur. The week of Memorial Day to June 1st, I remember numerous tests. I prayed silently that the hospital, the specialists, and God would get me through it. Instead of walking down the aisle at my wedding, I was in an elevator with my minister going up to the surgery floor. The minister and I prayed using Romans 12:12; God was watching over me. "To wait on the Lord and be patient in tribulation, trusting in His timing."

The surgery on my upper spine, or cervical 4-6, was to save my life. It was Saturday, June 1, 1985. My parents, grandparents, David, and others were in the waiting area. The surgeon, Dr. Kuecher, had come out to tell them that surgery went well and that I would be taken up to my room shortly. I was in the recovery room when I finally woke up. The recovery room nurses told me that I had died on the table for a few seconds, and they were not sure whether I was going to wake up.

During surgery, before waking up, I remembered a bright light and someone speaking to me that it was not time for me, and he had a plan. I went back to sleep and woke up in my private room. My dad was sitting in a chair next to the bed. He had been crying and was saying again that "his little girl was never going to walk again." I was groggy from the medication and the IV in my arm. The next morning, I took off the neck brace as well as the IV and decided I was going to walk to the bathroom. I got out of bed and went to the bathroom without a nurse's help. Still not realizing why I was in the hospital room, I made it back to my bed before my legs gave out, and I fell to the floor. A voice from a speaker yelled a code, and a red light flashed. I am not sure how I ended up in bed, but there I was.

Sunday morning, I was scared to move. I lay in bed as the physical therapist and occupational therapist came to evaluate me. The neurologist and orthopedic surgeon visited me and stated that the therapy would begin on Monday. Later that day, a psychologist and psychiatric evaluation took place. I asked my parents to bring me clothes, shoes, my cassette player, and my Howard Jones tape. I requested that the hospital staff no longer allow visitors. I did not need the extra stress, so I decided I had a job to do and did not need them there. At that time, I needed to learn patience so my body could heal.

The diagnosis was grim. The next week, walk with an assistive device, such as a walker, or learn to use a wheelchair. I had to accept my disability and that my strong will to live would provide the strength in this storm. The neck brace had to be worn all the time, and Dr. Kuecher was debating putting me into a Halo. I had seen another patient on my floor with this medical device called a Halo, and there was no way I was putting screws into my skull. One early morning during the second week of my hospital stay.

During Dr. Kuecher's visit, we talked about the Halo device. At that time, I told him I would listen diligently to the hospital staff and therapist. My physical therapy was two or three times a day, and occupational therapy every morning. My progress is walking more with a walker. Yet, at times, my body seemed like it did not want to cooperate. I continued to pray to God to help me heal and learn to be patient each day.

A favorite quote I try to say to myself even today. "Have patience with all things, but, chiefly first of all with yourself. Do not lose courage in considering your imperfections, but instead set remedying them-every day begin the task anew."[1]

I asked the hospital staff not to allow visits from family and friends. I had to work hard, both physically and mentally, to achieve my goal. Which was to walk again, and only I could do this. My release date was the Friday before the Fourth of July weekend. I would have my mom pick me up, then we would drive to the campground to spend a few weeks there before returning home. I still had sand embedded in my scalp. The surgeon would release me, but the plastic neck brace would be a cast, and I had to think about my future. I could live with my parents or get married. But I could not return to my college classes. It was almost the month of August, and the new wedding date had been set. As my patience with myself grew, so did my understanding of why, through my faith. Waiting, not always rushing, and slowing down provided me patience.

As you read this story, look into your soul and ask yourself: Do you have patience?

Are you in a storm of life because of an accident? Death, grieving, being born with a disability, or circumstances that you feel are out of your control? Pray to God because he does hear our prayers, and remember that no matter what you may be going through, God loves you. Until then, I hope that, whether you have physical or emotional challenges, you give yourself the patience to heal. The answer to prayers may be all around you, but you need to look, listen, and be patient.

The wedding had been postponed until late September 1985. I did not want my fiancée to feel sorry for me or feel obligated to marry me now because of my disabilities. I would wear the cast for four months, and it would come off right after Labor Day. I would wear a soft brace in the car until my yearly physical. In the spring of 1986, I would get the doctor's okay to return to college courses. Some of the courses were more challenging due to their physical demands. My major was early childhood with an emphasis on special needs. The more physical courses I took were incomplete, but the courses I thrived in helped maintain a B average. My husband David graduated in May 1986 and took employment in the suburbs of Chicago. We would pack up the U-Haul truck and the car with our dog, Mutton, and move again into an apartment in Naperville, Illinois. Here our life as a couple began. I started the process of finding the primary care providers and specialists covered by the company's medical plan. I soon overcame another challenge because my voice was hoarse and I had laryngitis most of the time. I needed to be tested for allergies.

My allergist contacted me by phone to let me know about many environmental and prescription allergies. This was new because I had never had allergies before the accident. I went weekly for allergy shots, one in each arm. This way, my body would build up an immunity to the allergens. We lived in Naperville for a year, then we looked for a starter home closer to my husband's workplace. We added a new member to our family by adopting a dog from an abusive situation. We found a house in Carpentersville, Illinois. The house had a fenced-in backyard, perfect for our dog Ubu. It had some work to be done inside, and I was up to the challenge to make this house our home. We found a local church to attend and became involved in its activities. We have been married for two years now. At this time, it felt like it was the right time to start a family. I still had some difficulty using my left hand and arm, but I had learned to adapt. The doctors were optimistic about the way I had improved, now able to walk and do more, but I would never be able to do any running or jogging. I was just thankful that I could do what I was doing as part of my normal routine. I would become pregnant with our first child. The doctors and specialists still did not know if I had any other damage internally from the accident.

A New Life

It was spring 1989 when our first child was born. We were excited to be new parents. I was twenty-five years old. Days were spent watching our little boy learn to make noises, sit up, turn over, crawl, say "mommy" or "daddy," pull himself up, and walk. When he was eight months old, I found out I was pregnant with our second child. I was excited, but my husband was not. He stated that the children were too close in age and asked me to abort the child. How could my husband ask me to do this? I was upset and crying. Later that day, I called my mom and asked her to listen, but she would not provide me with support. I decided that I could not do such a thing because God sent us another blessing.

My pregnancies were normal. I had morning sickness, weight gain, and some swollen feet. Most of my problems would be during the delivery. My legs would spasm, and I could only feel half of the contractions. After our second child was born in June 1990, I continued to go to my routine doctor appointments. The two children were healthy boys. We would stay busy with playgroups and mommy-and-baby swim classes. The oldest would attend preschool and library story time. Again, I would have issues with my legs and numerous spasms. The doctors would try medications like Lyrica, but my reactions would cause more side effects. I would eventually not take anything.

I decided to get a part-time job working at a donut shop at night to relieve some of the stress, and my leg spasms calmed down. I saved the money to go on vacation in July. The boys and I joined my parents on the Amtrak to travel to San Francisco. While we were there, we visited the redwood forest and the pier. Although we were with family, they did their schedule, so most of the time I was alone with the boys and had no help. When we returned home, I stopped working part-time because I had two young children who needed me. Also, David really did not like me working. He stated my job was to be at home. As I approached thirty, I decided to try one more time to get pregnant and try for a girl. We would get pregnant, but this time, I was bedridden for six months. I had to hire a part-time nanny. I hired a high school girl from our neighborhood to help me with the two boys in the evenings. My husband was working longer hours and was not home to help with the children's care. As my due date approached, I thought I was in labor. My ob/gyn was out of town for a seminar.

I was treated by the ob/gyn on call, and she stopped the contractions. When my ob/gyn returned, he was upset with the colleague who stopped my labor and fired her. One early morning, I went to see my ob/gyn, and the baby was not moving or kicking. The ob/gyn was concerned, so I started with caffeine and candy bars, but still no movement. I drank a can of cranberry juice, and wow, did the baby kick. The doctor asked me if I was ready to have a baby. He ordered an IV drip to start the labor, then an epidural injection to control the spasms.

During this time, medical technology was different, and so was health insurance. Labor was easier, and our daughter was born. I was then taken into surgery for tubal ligation and episionom, where I had torn during labor. I would be released to go in a few days, and a nurse would come to check on my stitches at our home.

During this time, I had three small children and thought our home was safe, until it was not. Our next-door neighbor would be shot. I felt violated when the police department went through our garbage and went through the toys in our backyard looking for the gun. I no longer felt safe and was worried about our children's safety. I began having anxiety attacks, not sleeping at night, and migraine headaches. My husband believed prescription drugs were the answer to all medical ailments. I believed that there were other solutions, including moving to a bigger home and a safer community.

The next step would be to move our family westward to northern Illinois. It was a small rural community surrounded by a lake. My parents came over to help with the children while we sold the Carpentersville house and signed the papers for the new home. It was a new construction home with a wooded backyard. We started the move. We would be busy planting native plants and doing yard work, putting up a wooden swing set, and settling into our new home. The boys were in preschool and kindergarten at the elementary school. We began going to the local Methodist church regularly. I joined the choir. We had the children registered in vacation bible school in the summer.

Sometimes accepting one's patience is a new beginning, while others deny it. My parents and family still have not accepted me with a disability, even though I struggle every day. Our society has taught us to label disabilities, diseases, or what is not normal as being swept under the rug. We judge others, and we do not show them patience.

"We do not want you to become lazy, but to imitate those through faith and patience inherit what has been promised" (Hebrews 6:12).

Takeaways

- Every morning, I took a few minutes to listen to the sounds around me. Now close your eyes and really listen. I always had a small notebook next to me.

- Journaling with adjectives to describe that moment or feeling.

- Reflect on your accomplishments from the day; this is where I learned patience.

- Look to God for help in developing patience with yourself.

Remember, God loves you and has patience with us. So, we too need to be patient with Him as he answers our big or small prayers. Learning to have patience at times can be challenging, but you can do it with God's guidance. We begin learning patience at an early age. Yet, we do not understand the true meaning until a storm in our lives takes place. No matter what you, as an individual, might be going through, you are not alone. My journey made me learn patience.

"Patience leads to abundant understanding, but impatience leads to stupid mistakes" (Proverbs 14:29-30; CEB). Yes, I made the mistake of diving into the lake, and even as my medical journey continued through my adult life. I still have challenges. Even today, I listen to music from Howard Jones. My favorites are "There Is No One to Blame" and "Things Can Only Get Better." I do not blame God for my problems but embrace them. I am now on permanent disability. I have accepted my limitations and continue to follow my purpose by helping others or providing joy to others. I believe that I am continuing to learn about myself. I am no longer an alcoholic and have been sober for three years. Do not get me wrong, there have been times I wanted to grab a bottle for a drink. Since my divorce in 2019, I now realize that drinking my pain physically or emotionally away is not the answer. Tomorrow is a new day.

Chapter 6

Patience: Getting to the Joyful End

By Kelly Higdon

I AM STILL CONFIDENT OF THIS: I WILL SEE THE GOODNESS OF THE LORD IN THE LAND OF THE LIVING. WAIT FOR THE LORD; BE STRONG AND TAKE HEART AND WAIT FOR THE LORD.
-PSALM 27:13-14

In August 1999, I was 28 years old and single. I had arrived in Bouake, Côte d'Ivoire, West Africa, to begin working as a dorm assistant at the International Christian Academy. This boarding school served missionary families ministering in West Africa. I had spent the previous years completing the steps to serve overseas with my denomination; I had obtained a 4-year degree and had 2+ years of working in a local church. The French language training would come later, but the opportunity to serve the amazing children of missionaries was a dream come true, and it (gratefully) required only English while on campus. I had waited and prayed for years for this opportunity, for God to make clear the details of what serving Him might look like overseas. It was a privilege to now be part of the staff at the school that

I had heard so much about. I served with a married couple in one of the eight school dormitories on campus. In our dorm alone, we had 24 students ranging from second to eighth grade. While each school year would bring its fair share of changes among students and new and returning staff members, the school had known such a protective experience from political upheaval until then.

While I was getting used to my first four months in country, which included encountering bugs of unusual size, incredible sub-Saharan heat, and power outages, Côte d'Ivoire experienced its first *coup d'etat*. The events that occurred on Christmas Eve, when the sitting president was replaced by another, filled that day with distant gunfire and mixed reactions among some staff members. The coup occurred when students were back with their families during the Christmas Break. There didn't seem to be any local effect or danger afterward for those of us who lived 5 hours from the capital city of Abidjan. Students returned to school. The political tension in the country, though, did cause school leaders to enhance security by beginning construction of a 10-foot-high concrete wall around the 26 acres of our campus. While Côte d'Ivoire was changing, ICA had provided vital educational services for thousands of missionary children for over 30 years.

Like the familiar adage about a frog boiling in water, the country's political climate seemed to add new degrees of risk. More and more stories were being relayed to us about carjackings and even kidnappings. After each political incident, peace and stability seemed to return to normal again, with some minor changes in additional security.

Perhaps due to the increasing political turmoil, crime was on the rise. New security measures were introduced. Then, on July 17, 2002, armed robbers entered our campus, murdered Soro, one of our security guards, and kidnapped our business manager, Mike Cousineau. Mike miraculously escaped and returned to campus. Following the robbery and the shock, the staff gathered and prayed, believing that God wanted our school to stay open. We dedicated the 2002-2003 school year with renewed faith to be committed to God's timing and purposes. Missionary families cautiously brought their children back to school to begin the new school year. Six weeks after the robbery, the unthinkable happened.

As believers, we are called to know Christ and make Him known. When a Christian senses God's leading into ministry, seldom does the whole picture become visible. Patience and perseverance partner to prepare one for ministry. Rarely will anyone foresee the relationships that will be forged from serving with others. Prior to the mass use of the internet, cell phones, and social media, when there was greater isolation from families of origin, the missionary community was very much like a family formed by the unique reasons that brought them to serve cross-culturally. Those who have known something of patience and perseverance can form a bond, especially in times of pain and loss.

On September 18th, 2002, a beloved member of our school's dorm staff, Dave Golding, died suddenly during a run on the school's track. The immediacy of this event was deeply shocking for his wife, Denise, their three children, their dorm full of middle school boys, and our entire campus of 200 students and staff members. Before we had even had a full day to absorb this occurrence, news of political turmoil was reaching our campus. The national workers on campus were huddled around radios, anxiously listening to French news reports. A red flag warning had been posted at the gate, alerting us that no one should plan to go into town. In the local residential community, some gunfire could be heard. By September 20th, our school campus had been surrounded by the two main factions in the uprising.[1] For the next 6 days, our campus was "locked down" at different times, as we were positioned in the crosshairs of Cote d'Ivoire's civil war, opposite factions using the walls of our campus as their barricades. At the end of six days, a ceasefire had been arranged, French and American special forces had entered our story and arranged for our entire student body and staff to be escorted to the capital city of Abidjan, where students were reunited with their waiting parents, and leaders from various missions met with the staff for debriefing. Upon the completion of these meetings, each staff member had to ponder what would come next for the ministry, then inform mission leadership.

I had spent years preparing and anticipating serving the Lord overseas. I did not want to return to the United States. I wanted to stay with the others, who were preparing to go to Dakar Academy in Senegal. While I was clear about what I wanted, I was void of peace. As the minutes ticked towards my meeting time, a seemingly irrelevant question kept creeping into my mind: *What did Jesus say to the man who had been healed of a legion of demons?* The question replayed in my mind with increased intensity, to the point of needing to look up the text prior to my meeting. Within a few minutes, I found my Bible and read the answer to the persistent question: "Return home and tell how much God has done for you." (Luke 8:39a).

My journey in Africa ended that week. As I reflect on my time leading up to serving at the International Christian Academy, my few years there, and then the twenty-something years since, there has been much to suggest God often uses time to reshape the experience of knowing Him. Practicing patience is a rare opportunity to stay connected to the One who loves us and calls us to show His love to others. Patience was an important component of embracing what God had permitted. Most would agree that left to our own devices, patience is a difficult virtue to acquire. While everyone agrees that patience is a virtue, some might downplay the significance of actively seeking to obtain and develop this virtue as a vital component of faithful living. Was it possible to have assurance of God's care when I did not know the next phase of His plan? In the time since, my question slowly changed into other questions. I have accepted that patience had less to do with my wants, my goals, and my roles in this life. Rather, patience had more to do with these three ambitions: knowing God's presence, witnessing His work, and responding to His ultimate desire to call us Home.

Patience is evidence of God's Presence.

Before the beginning of Creation, God was. Time and process were God's inventions right alongside all other things for man and woman to govern. As God's image bearers, Adam and Eve, before the Fall, lived the fruitful life mentioned in Galatians 5:22-23, as they were graced with God's presence. It is ironic, perhaps, that they should then experience such brokenness by sampling a different fruit they were expressly told not to eat. With disobedience came the fall from grace. Chaos, sin, and separation wrenched the Creator from his beloved creation, spoiling the good fruit amply supplied to our first parents. Only through the redemption of Christ, could such fruit be renewed and flourish once again as the Holy Spirit fills those who belong to God. "...the fruit of the Spirit is love, joy, peace, *patience*, kindness, goodness, faithfulness, gentleness and self-control. Against such things there is no law." (Galatians 5:22-23, emphasis added). In our broken and troubled world, it is tempting to think that it is our job to do the best we can, to obey, and manufacture all kinds of spiritual strength on our own to do big things, go to faraway places, and do the heroic thing, like being patient. What a relieving thought to know that this troubling burden does not originate within us but has been gifted through the renewing work of the Holy Spirit. Patience does not originate from our brokenness, but from God's presence in our lives.

As one considers patience, one can see, as David did, that it often invites God's activity into our circumstances. Consider Psalm 40:1, "I waited patiently for the LORD; he turned to me and heard my cry." The remaining psalm portrays the worshipful response to God, who engages with the recipients He loves. To those who love God, patience reveals God's presence among them.

Peter also taught us much about patience, more often than not, by the many ways he was corrected by the Lord, before the Lord's crucifixion. Later, in Peter's writing to believers, something powerful is communicated about patience. It is not just a practice and a gift for believers, but an experience that God has with us. "The Lord is not slow in keeping his promise, as some understand slowness. Instead, he is patient with you, not wanting anyone to perish, but everyone to come to repentance." (2 Peter 3:9). Oh, how the Father loves and wants people to know Him!

When I think of my time at the International Christian Academy, I am grateful to see how the school leaders turned to God, fully relying on God's presence, His protection, and direction. They were patiently waiting on God while they actively served. They met together and communicated regular updates to mission leaders who had missionary families serving in the western part of the continent and whose children we had within our walls. When news agencies and concerned parties in the US began reaching out to them, they appointed a public information officer among the teachers on campus to address inquiries. At one point, I was contacted to see about creating space for possibly 1,000 members of the expat community living nearby to join us on campus. Others were tasked with siphoning fuel from all non-essential vehicles to power the main generator on campus when the electricity was cut from town. Teachers were preparing lessons to help keep children on track throughout the day. The director of food services miraculously kept us all fed throughout that week from what was stored on campus. With a thousand moving parts and plenty of uncertainty, the leaders personified patience as they dispensed God's ample grace to us. One of my treasures from my time in Africa was a batik picture, made through the beautiful dying process of wax, colored dyes, and canvas, depicting a smiling African boy holding up five small fish and two loaves of bread. Upon such a remembrance of our lockdown week, I think of the smiling child in the picture and of our gracious God who supplied the needs of the masses, even in the few winks of sleep and amid all the human limitations in the midst of the trouble we knew.

Patience reveals God's redemptive work in His creation.

This point can feel particularly harsh. *Why do bad things happen to good people?* Such a question can easily be asked when the news amply provides reports of murders, exploitation, or even turmoil surrounding a school for missionary children. But the question can reveal a hidden accusation. *God, why are You not doing what is expected of You?* When believers act patiently, they step into the existing work of God, in which hearts, minds, and motives are revealed. Perhaps it is not the waiting that makes people resistant to the concept of patience, but the discomfort of exposure that almost always occurs when we are thwarted in our expectations. Paul taught the Romans that, as believers in Christ, they were free from sin, which resulted in holiness (Romans 6:22-23). This personal sanctification means that believers are not God, but they experience the newness of God's nature, restoring us to what He originally wanted for us. We were not intended to be God but to be redeemed by God to His original intent. With such, the tone of my questions towards God is no longer hiding accusation but honestly reflects my powerlessness and my need for the answer-holding God.

After the lockdown week and our evacuation, and in the moments leading up to the meeting with mission leaders, I can still remember the sticky, humid air, where I sat in the mission guesthouse playground, and the searing urgency of the question that led me to Luke 8. I imagined how I might answer the following question: *Kelly, where do you sense God is leading you now that you will never be returning to the International Christian Academy?* I wanted to be poised, determined, and enthusiastically on board with going to Dakar Academy with my other co-worker. They needed a single woman to assist in the dorm. *I... was. . .needed. . .*oh, what trouble had often been started by responding to such magical words with rushed-into "yeses." As it turned out, the mission leaders were more tactful in querying my intent. They had a critical role in returning children to their parents, debriefing many of their team members, determining how best to address the trauma of the missionaries and their children, and addressing ministry focus in Côte d'Ivoire, all while managing the resources entrusted to them. I remain incredibly grateful for such godly leadership during that difficult time. Nonetheless, after my meeting where I reported my intent to return to the U.S., I had a one-way ticket back to Los Angeles, no job, no ministry, a backpack containing all my earthly belongings, and no understanding of what would come next. The new mission was to return home and tell how much God had done for me. This new mission was not the one I had in mind.

I was 31, returning to the white-and-gold princess-style furniture in my childhood bedroom in my parents' home and reconnecting with my family and friends. I bought a bus pass to commute to my little job at a bank. I rode with the same people regularly, and we would share looks and common greetings that expressed at least some familiarity. They did not know they were helping me return to a normal life. I had been so lavishly blessed, with time to heal and only the simplicity of a bus ride and a job to handle.

Additionally, my experience was difficult to translate to others. Still, in returning to my parents' home, I was able to connect with my father, with whom I had a strained relationship. My Christian faith and interest in ministry baffled him. He had other words for it. But now, back at home, my dad began to share his experience in Vietnam as a young Marine. In a year, I bought a car. I met John, my future husband (my pilot man). We married in December 2003. In 2010, we adopted a precious 4-year-old, Mark. Then in 2017, we adopted our second son, Tyler, who was 10 years old, 3 months older than our first son. With John's work, we moved from the High Desert in Southern California to the flatlands of South Florida, to the beautiful foothills of western North Carolina. I had several jobs and ministry opportunities. With all these transitions, I had fresh opportunities to exercise patience. Romans 5:1-8 reminds me that faith has come from both hope and suffering. With new locations come stories of meeting people from all walks of life, many of whom have shared their own stories of God's saving grace.

Patience transitions us from our current circumstances to our eventual Home.

Following the 6 days of lockdown, when all the staff had gathered to debrief, a wise counselor asked us to build a timeline of events. All were invited to contribute their experience. By the end of that beautiful session, the 35 or so of us who were able to attend this session had a deep understanding of all that had transpired during those six days. There were tears, there was shared language and connection, and fears were named and addressed. The grace and protection we had known was nothing less than the inner workings of the Kingdom of Heaven in the midst of hell. I didn't know at that point that that meeting would be the last time I would see most of my fellow staff members. In the meantime, we have connected through social media and occasional run-ins at weddings, conferences, and home assignments. It's not the same. There have been other circumstances when I had a defined time of connection, such as youth conferences, deep talks with friends at my college, and a young adult group at my church. Nowadays, when I reflect on all such moments, I realize that the longing and nostalgia I experience were the moments I sensed God's presence whispering to me to look towards Eternity. God's presence in times of suffering reminds us that we are preparing for an eternal home. Trouble, hardship, and trauma are the experiences of the economy of this present world alone. Grace, power, and overcoming are in God's Kingdom, His economy. Patience allows me to exchange my earthly currency before my final destination.

In the course of life, there are surely more appealing virtues that are more easily attained, that have a more material-like base of evidence of spiritual growth. Patience is hard to quantify or measure; it is a little abstract and subject to interpretation. It is difficult to practice and check for growth. Perhaps then it is good news that we are not the chief adjudicator in determining the growth of our spiritual condition. Spiritual growth is not determined by man but by God (1 Samuel 16:7).

My days in Africa are long over. My brief experience living across cultures made me all too aware of my lack of patience, especially without air-conditioning, with crowds around me in marketplaces, and with the lack of availability of an icy-cold Diet Pepsi. Learning to sleep through the imagined (or perhaps not imagined) crawling sensations that made me think a bug was on me, drinking plenty of clean water, and getting regular exercise helped me acclimate to the new stresses in my new home. Still, nothing fortified my spirit like a regular time in God's word, worshipping in song, and journaling. These disciplines led to other opportunities like becoming a Sunday School teacher, offering to organize and inventory curriculum, making lunch seating charts that would need to be rotated every two weeks, chairing school banquet planning meetings, all of which became the small acts of service that were helpful to keep seeing others over my own irritations and shortcomings. I did not grow patience, but it grew in me while I was working on other things. If it is true that in this world we are to have trouble, then we can take heart, because Jesus has overcome the world (John 16:33). A big part of "taking heart" is living according to the Spirit.

Father, what might I do today to honor You, serve another, get over my crankiness, my fear, my irritation? I need help walking in the Spirit, what are the tangible ways I can do this? Rescue me from the need to have things my way, in my time, and on my terms? How would you have me be? In Jesus' name, Your will, not mine, be done. Amen.

When we know God, though we do not know what to do, where to go, or how to be in any given circumstance, the answers we receive are from our patient God. He wants us to become more like Him. In the non-battling moments, we can store up truth, we sharpen our knowledge of God's word, and we smooth our unruly spiritual cowlicks with love and discipline. We gather patience when the Spirit responds to the agency we take. We receive the fruit of patience, as all other skills, when we live lives that are under the command of Christ. As quoted before: "The Lord is not slow in keeping his promise, as some understand slowness. He is patient with you, not wanting anyone to perish, but everyone to come to repentance" (2 Peter 3:9). What happens when I pray for patience? I became positioned to understand that God is "bigger" than me. He is sovereign, omniscient, active, a keeper of details, and effective with prompts. When I know He is truly all these things, the pressure can be off to try to be all these things. The result means I am less frantic, more patient. I can be protected and empowered when I am not worried about being the redeemer in the moment. I can work with others, share in the emotions of the group, and keep a clear mind. I will not be lost, forgotten, or forsaken. I need not wonder what God would have for me to do. In our patient God, we can be prayerful and keep a clear eye on the days ahead.

It is my hope that my circumstances in the fall of 2002 presented a clear model of how patience is a gift, meant to guide me throughout my life and prepare me for that sweet day when I will step out of this life and enter into Eternity. This matters for the believer who needs to reconsider patience as a means to sensing God's invitation. God is present, and He is working to welcome us Home.

Next Steps

Meditate on the words of this beautiful hymn. The German hymnwriter Katharina von Schlegel wrote it in the 1750s. Very little is known about her. Later, the hymn was translated by British hymn writer Jane Borthwick in 1854. For today, it serves as a timely reminder that being patient has been an age-old challenge, but at the final edge, our patience will no longer be required. The hard work will be done.

> Be still my soul, the Lord is on thy side;
>
> Bear patiently, the cross of grief and shame.
>
> Leave to thy God to order or provide;
>
> In every change He faithful will remain.
>
> Be still my soul, thy best, thy heavenly Friend
>
> Through thorny ways leads to a joyful end.[2]

Chapter 7

Patience: The Father I Found While Waiting for Her

By Jennifer Jackson

FOR MY THOUGHTS ARE NOT YOUR THOUGHTS, NEITHER ARE YOUR WAYS MY WAYS, DECLARES THE LORD. FOR AS THE HEAVENS ARE HIGHER THAN THE EARTH, SO ARE MY WAYS HIGHER THAN YOUR WAYS AND MY THOUGHTS THAN YOUR THOUGHTS.
FOR AS THE RAIN AND THE SNOW COME DOWN FROM HEAVEN AND DO NOT RETURN THERE BUT WATER THE EARTH, MAKING IT BRING FORTH AND SPROUT, GIVING SEED TO THE SOWER AND BREAD TO THE EATER, SO SHALL MY WORD BE THAT GOES OUT FROM MY MOUTH; IT SHALL NOT RETURN TO ME EMPTY, BUT IT SHALL ACCOMPLISH THAT WHICH I PURPOSE, AND SHALL SUCCEED IN THE THING FOR WHICH I SENT IT.
- ISAIAH 55:8-11, ESV

The Breaking Point

I encountered God and the spirit realm early, at four years old. Even then, my spirit bore witness to the Truth. But at night, terror gripped me.

I could see spiritual things that others couldn't. I watched my mother spiral. I watched my sister shrink under the weight of it all. And I was powerless to stop any of it.

That's when I reached a terrifying conclusion: I needed to kill them to set them free.

In the 80s and 90s, talking about spiritual warfare at home—fighting demons both literally and metaphorically—was taboo, even for some Christians. People who saw such things were thought to be "sick" or "crazy." Trying to articulate these experiences sounded insane, even to those living them.

So I learned to suffer in silence, waiting for something to change, though I didn't know what or when.

By my teenage years, I'd learned how to fight my own demons. But I had no idea how to fight the ones destroying my mother.

She lived as if everything was fine when others were around. Her darkness emerged only when no one else was there to witness the evil things she said.

How do you kill what you can see but can't touch? How do you save someone who doesn't know they need saving?

That's what I wrote in my notebook. The question I couldn't ask out loud: "How do I kill my mother and my sister?"

I never meant for her to find it.

But she did.

I was napping in her bed when she woke me. My eyes opened slowly, still heavy with sleep, and for a second, I couldn't understand what was happening. She was sitting on the floor below me, her face unreadable.

"I read your notebook," she said. Her voice was flat, careful. "Do you really want to kill your sister and me?"

The grogginess evaporated instantly. The air felt different—heavy, like something had already shattered between us and we were just waiting to see how bad the damage was.

I couldn't look at her, so I stared at the wall behind her head.

"Yes."

The word came out quieter than I meant it to, but it was the truth. The only truth I had.

"That's how I really feel."

Silence.

But not the empty kind. This silence had weight—the kind that sits on your chest. She looked up at me from the floor, and what I saw in her eyes wasn't understanding. It was fear. Confusion. Like she'd just discovered I was someone she didn't recognize—someone terrifying she couldn't name.

Then she finally spoke.

"Wow. Okay. Wow."

That's all she said. Just *wow*. Like my confirmation had knocked every other word out of her head.

But here's what broke me: she didn't ask why. She didn't ask what was happening to me. She just heard my answer and shut down.

She didn't see me at all.

She didn't see a child trapped in a spiritual war she didn't understand. She didn't see a daughter who'd been fighting demons since she was four years old. She didn't see the desperation of watching her mother be oppressed by darkness—or a child who had no idea how to save her.

She just heard "I want to kill you" and couldn't get past the words to see the spiritual crisis underneath.

That's the real tragedy of that moment. Not what I said, but that I was completely alone in it.

I was a frustrated teenager armed with nothing but desperation and a conviction that something had to change. No one had taught me how to truly destroy the works of Satan. So I defaulted to the only solution that made sense to a child drowning in spiritual darkness: eliminate the source.

But God saw me in that darkness. That very summer, when I was fourteen years old and staying with my auntie, He stepped in and showed me exactly who He was—and who I was to Him.

I was stuck in this cycle—anger boiling up, lashing out, no one to turn to when the world felt unjust. Just rage and desperation and a fourteen-year-old girl who didn't know how to break free. But God was working in the background on my behalf.

Summer of '94 - Heart Check

I'm fourteen, staying with my auntie for the summer, and God corners me.

Not in a vision. Not in a dream. Just His voice, clear as day, cutting through everything else.

"You have a lot of anger inside you."

I know. Of course I know. I've been carrying it for years—this lead shot lodged in my chest, heavy and hot.

"Would you like to know where it stems from?"

I don't even hesitate. "Oh, I know where it stems from. That woman You gave me as a mother—that's where it stems from."

Silence.

Then: *"You're wrong."*

I stop. The ground shifts. Wrong? How could I be wrong? She's the one who—

"Your anger doesn't stem from your mother. It stems from you being a fatherless child. An orphan. You have no one else to consult with when you believe your mother is making unfair and unjust decisions. That's what angers you."

I stand there, stunned. Fatherless. Orphan. The words settle over me like a diagnosis I didn't know I needed.

And the very next morning, God proves His point.

A memory surfaces—standing at the kitchen sink before dawn, forced to wash dishes that aren't even mine. It's not my turn. I *know* it's not my turn. But there I am anyway, hands in soapy water, and something inside me snaps.

The anger that's been simmering underneath for so long suddenly boils over—hot, fierce, uncontrollable. I'm furious at the unfairness of it, at being treated like I don't matter, at having no one to appeal to, no father to say, *"Wait, is this right?"*

I grab one of those dishes and try to break it. I really try. I want to smash it, to destroy something, to give this rage somewhere to go.

But the dish won't break.

I try again. And again. My hands are shaking, my chest is heaving, and the anger is pouring out of me—but the dishes just won't break.

I stand there gripping that plate, feeling the full force of my rage with nowhere for it to land. And that's when I see it clearly: this anger isn't just a feeling. It's a force. And when someone provokes it, it erupts as pure, desperate destruction.

The dishes won't break, which only makes me angrier. I finish washing them all, then crawl back to bed to squeeze in a little more sleep before school.

But I can't stop thinking about what God said. *Fatherless. Orphan.*

Over the next few days, He keeps showing me my heart. When I'm around friends who have their fathers in their lives, I feel it—not jealousy toward them, but this raw, aching question: *Why didn't my father want me?*

That's the anger. Not my mother. My father's rejection. The unknown of it. The unanswered *why.*

Then God gives me a poem. I don't know where it comes from—it just flows out of me, words I didn't know I had. It's a release. A letting go of my earthly dad. I write it down, read it to a few people, and place it on the desk in my room.

The next morning, it's gone.

I searched everywhere. Under the bed, in drawers, between books. I ask my aunt and uncle if they've seen it. They haven't. They even help me look.

After searching for a while, I gave up. I close the bedroom door behind me and stand there, frustrated and confused.

"God," I say out loud, "did You see it?"

He doesn't answer with a yes or no.

Instead, He asks me a question. A question that changed my life forever.

"Will you allow Me to be your Heavenly Father?"

I don't think. I don't hesitate. I don't weigh the implications.

I just say, "Yes."

The moment that word leaves my mouth, something shifts. An inexplicable joy floods through me—something I still can't fully explain. It's not happiness. It's deeper than that. It's belonging. It's being seen. It's being chosen.

That yes launches a journey with God I didn't know I needed.

And that poem? I'm convinced an angel of the Most High took it during the night to completely free me from it.

God Wants to Be Your Heavenly Father

Let me pause here and talk to you for a second.

Maybe you're reading this, and you have a father, but he's absent in the ways that matter. Or maybe, like me, you grew up with a void so deep you didn't even have words for it.

Here's what I learned that summer at 14: God doesn't just want to be God to you—distant, untouchable, theological. He wants to be your Father. Your Abba. The one who fills every gap your earthly parents left behind.

But here's the thing—you've got to say yes. You've got to invite Him into that specific role in your life. It's not automatic. He extends the invitation, and you have to respond.

When I said yes that day, I didn't fully understand what I was agreeing to. I just knew I was tired. Tired of the anger. Tired of feeling unwanted.

If you've never done this, I want you to consider it right now. Ask God to be your Heavenly Father. Not just your Savior, not just your Lord, but your Father. The one who sees you, knows you, and will never reject you.

This is where your healing begins—by claiming your identity as His beloved child.

This was the first seed God planted in my heart. But seeds don't become trees overnight. They require time, watering, and the patience to trust the process even when you can't see what's happening beneath the soil.

Here's what I didn't understand then: having God as my Father didn't mean my circumstances would immediately change. It meant I finally had someone who could see me—really see me—spiritually and emotionally in ways my mother never could.

In the Midst of It All

When summer break ended, I came home expecting everything to feel different.

It didn't.

The same dynamics were there. The same tension. The same pain. And for a moment, I felt confused—if God had done something so real in me, why hadn't my environment changed?

Because transformation doesn't begin around you. It begins within you.

But the enemy didn't like that I'd found peace, so he escalated. My mother's words grew sharper. My sister grew darker. And everything in me wanted to fight back.

So I did. My tongue became my weapon. When she hurled hurtful words, I fired back with cutting remarks. All the while dying inside, crying silently in my room or to my oldest sister.

I was waiting for things to get better. Waiting for my mother to change. Waiting for the pain to stop.

But I didn't yet understand that waiting without patience is just suffering with a different name.

So, I ran. At 18, I married my way out of that house, thinking escape was the same as healing. I left home believing that distance would finally give me what God promised. Peace, belonging, and a father's love.

It didn't work that way.

Our relationship didn't improve—if anything, it grew worse. I began questioning God about why He gave me two unloving parents who clearly didn't want me. I felt rejected, unloved, abandoned, alone, and unlovable.

What I didn't know was that God saw me, heard me, and cared for me. He was still working, still moving, still preparing me for what He knew I needed.

But I had to learn to wait on His timeline, not mine.

Here's where things get complicated—and honestly, where the real transformation started. Because sometimes God has to take you somewhere completely new to show you something you couldn't see where you were.

The NYC Turning Point (The Pastor's Office)

By now, I was living in NYC with my husband and two children. God laid a church on my heart—one He wanted me to attend.

After three months of fighting it, I finally took my family there. It was absolutely the place we needed, and we should've gone much sooner.

I became active, attending different classes and Bible studies. I was growing in truth in ways I never thought possible.

One Tuesday morning, the women's pastor called me. She asked if I could meet her before our weekly Bible study to talk about something important.

After some small talk, she looked at me and asked, out of nowhere, "How is your relationship with your mom?"

I was immediately annoyed. At this point in my life, I was done.

"It sucks," I told her flatly. "I wouldn't even call it a relationship. She's just my mom, and I'm just her daughter. Why do you ask?"

"Well, I believe God placed it on my heart to talk to you about it," she said gently. "He wants you to surrender your relationship over to Him."

My beautiful "Christian" response was anything but holy. "You've got to be kidding me, right? Why does He care? He's the one who gave her to me! I'm done with her. I don't want a relationship with her anymore. It's too painful being her daughter."

The pastor gave me "The Look"—the one that needs no introduction and certainly no explanation.

I threw a quick tantrum, then sighed.

"I don't even know how to do that," I admitted. "What does surrender even look like?"

She grabbed my hands. "I've been where you are," she said softly. "Surrender is giving up your way for His. It looks like shutting your mouth when He tells you to, no matter how badly you want to speak. It looks like stopping when He says stop and going when He says go."

After she prayed for me, I told her I'd do my best and asked her to keep praying for me.

The Refined Lesson: Waiting vs. Patience

So this new journey with my mother began—though she had no idea how dramatically things were about to shift.

This transformation didn't happen overnight. It took years for things to even start improving. And in those years, God didn't waste a single moment.

He wasted no time testing this new surrender.

I was in my mid-20s and needed to quit my job at Macy's. When I called my mom to talk about it, I wasn't met with encouragement. Instead, she told me, "I always quit at everything and would amount to nothing at this rate."

I heard the Holy Spirit say, "End the call."

After a brief pause, I did. Then I bawled my eyes out. I cried so hard because I couldn't give her a piece of my mind like I wanted to.

God knew best, and I didn't have to repent.

PRAISE ELOHIM!

The Difference Between Waiting and Patience

Throughout this pruning process, God showed me things that shifted my entire perspective. He taught me that having patience isn't the same as waiting. And I need you to hear this because it changed everything for me.

I realized that, for many of us, "waiting" is a mask we wear to avoid taking action. It's a stagnant state where we marinate in our pain and pray it dissolves on its own. We say, "I'm waiting on God," but what we really mean is, "I'm paralyzed and don't know what to do, so I'm calling it waiting."

We're not actively trusting; we're numbing ourselves with inaction.

But patience? Patience is completely different.

Patience is active anticipation.

It's the expectation that God will do exactly what He said He would do. Patience says, "I don't see it yet, but I know it's coming because God promised."

Patience keeps you engaged in the process, keeps you obedient in the waiting, keeps you surrendered even when nothing seems to be changing.

Let this truth settle into your heart: Some of us trust God, but we don't wait on Him very well. We believe He can do it, but we struggle to wait for Him to do it in His timing.

I had to learn that trusting God to keep His promise is the foundation, but waiting on Him to fulfill it is the discipline.

Here's what patience looked like for me practically:

- It meant ending phone calls when the Holy Spirit prompted me, even when I wanted to defend myself.
- It meant praying for my mother when I wanted to curse her.
- It meant showing up to family events when I wanted to isolate.
- It meant choosing forgiveness over and over again, even when she didn't ask for it or deserve it.

Patience wasn't passive. It was the hardest, most active work I've ever done.

And here's what I learned: Patience doesn't just change your circumstances—it changes you. While I was waiting for my mother to change, God was using patience to transform my heart. He was teaching me how to love as He loves. How to forgive as He forgives. How to see people through His eyes instead of through my wounds.

Throughout this season, God Almighty taught me how to love Him better than myself and others. This was huge for me because I didn't realize I wasn't loving others well until I experienced my Heavenly Father's love firsthand.

During those years in NYC, God was so intentional about healing my broken heart and freeing me from the "mother wounds" I'd carried for decades. He strategically placed a woman in my life—my "NY Mom"—to show me the motherly love I'd missed. I'm so grateful to God for always knowing what I need and when I need it.

Surrender Is the Pathway to Transformation

I thought surrender meant giving up—walking away clean, protecting myself, cutting off the pain at the source.

But God said no.

His thoughts aren't my thoughts. His ways aren't my ways (Isaiah 55:8, ESV).

Here's what I know now: Surrender isn't defeat. It's choosing God's way over your way, even when His way doesn't make sense yet. It's the daily decision to give Him your timeline, your expectations, your desired outcomes, and your pain.

Surrender and patience work together. You can't truly surrender without patience, and you can't develop patience without surrender. They're inseparable—both requiring you to trust God more than you trust your own understanding.

Because I surrendered my timeline to His, my mother and I now have a relationship I never imagined possible. I was severely wounded, but God stepped in. He didn't just want me to survive the relationship; He wanted me to receive my full portion of healing. He accomplished what He desired. GLORY BE TO ALMIGHTY GOD!

And He will do the same for you.

Your Invitation to Healing

I'm sharing my story so the right woman or child who's now an adult hears this: God wants to step in and change your situation, too.

Maybe you're reading this, and you see yourself in my story. Maybe you have a mother who wounded you, or maybe you are the mother who inflicted the wounds. Maybe you're carrying anger that's been lodged in your heart for decades, or maybe you're stuck in that passive "waiting" stage, hoping things will magically get better without doing the hard work of surrender and patience.

I want you to know something: God sees you. He hasn't forgotten about you. And He's inviting you into the same journey He took me on—a journey of healing, transformation, and relationships that seem impossible to be restored.

But it starts with a choice.

Three choices, actually.

First, you've got to say yes to God being your Heavenly Father.

Invite Him into that specific role. Let Him fill the voids your earthly parents left. Let Him love you the way you've always needed to be loved. This is your foundation.

Second, you've got to surrender your timeline and your desired outcome to Him.

Stop trying to control how and when healing happens. Stop trying to force people to change on your schedule. Give it all to God—the pain, the anger, the relationship, the timeline—and trust that His ways are higher than yours.

Third, you've got to learn the difference between waiting and patience.

Stop being passive in your pain. Start actively anticipating what God's going to do. Stay obedient in the process. Keep showing up. Keep forgiving. Keep loving. Keep trusting. That's patience—and patience transforms you while you wait for your circumstances to change.

Whether you're the mother who inflicted the wounds or the child who received them, ask God for strength and endurance. Don't pray for patience—it'll come and increase daily through surrender and obedience.

My relationship with my mother is far from perfect, but I now see her through God's eyes. I see her differently. I love her from a healed, whole heart instead of a broken, wounded one. I can love her well because I love Him more.

God loved me out of death and brought me back to life. He can do the same for your pain.

Hebrews 6:15 (ESV) says: "And thus Abraham, having patiently waited, obtained the promise."

Let me leave you with this: Abraham waited 25 years for the promise God gave him. Twenty-five years of active patience. Twenty-five years of trusting when nothing looked like it was changing. Twenty-five years of surrender. And then, at exactly the right time—God's time, not Abraham's—the promise came.

Your promise is coming too. But the question is, will you wait well? Will you let patience do her perfect work in you while you wait? Will you surrender your way for His?

I'm praying that you will. I'm praying that you'll say yes to the Father, yes to surrender, and yes to patience. Because on the other side of that "yes" is a healing you can't even imagine yet.

Let's learn to wait well while patience does her perfect work, so we can see the promise together.

Your healing isn't just possible—it's already promised.

Now let's step into it together, one surrendered, patient moment at a time.

Chapter 8

Letters to Timothy: Surrendering the Legacy to the God of the Long Wait

By Elizabeth Clark

BEING CONFIDENT OF THIS VERY THING, THAT HE WHO HAS BEGUN A GOOD WORK IN YOU WILL COMPLETE IT UNTIL THE DAY OF JESUS CHRIST.
- PHILIPPIANS 1:6, NKJV

The Day The World Bent

Trauma rarely announces itself. On September 26, 2017, it arrived disguised as a completely ordinary, gray Wednesday morning. My sweet fourteen-year-old son, Timothy, was in the passenger seat of our Jeep. We were driving toward Mansfield Christian School, chatting idly about his upcoming math test and what we were having for dinner. I was behind the wheel, my eyes on the road, entirely secure in the illusion of our safe, predictable life.

And then, a scream of metal.

A dark-blue Durango veered violently into our lane. There was absolutely no time to brace or react. The impact was deafening, a sound that wasn't just heard, but felt deep in the marrow of my bones. In a fraction of a second, the world bent out of control. Glass rained down over us like jagged diamonds as the dashboard crumpled inward, trapping us in the wreckage.

When the Jeep finally spun to a halt, the silence was heavy, choked with the bitter smell of burning rubber and deployed airbags. I instantly realized I was pinned against the steering wheel. I couldn't move my right arm; it lay limp and unresponsive. Blinding waves of pain washed over me, crushing my arm and my ankle.

Worse than the pain was the panic. I couldn't turn my head to see Timothy. Moaning and gripping my chest with my good hand, I gasped for air.

LETTER 1: The Smoke and the Pact

September 29, 2017. OhioHealth Mansfield Hospital, Recovery Room

Dearest Timothy,

I am just drifting awake from surgery, typing this with my left hand, the only part of my body that still seems to obey. My right arm is trapped in a heavy cast, and my foot is wrapped in bandages. But of all my broken pieces, my heart aches the most because you are miles away in a different hospital.

I am replaying those long minutes in the wreckage. I remember the suffocating weight of my own powerlessness. As a mother, my hands have always been the tools I use to fix your world, cook your meals, tousle your hair, and steady you when you trip. But in that mangled Jeep, my hands were useless. One was pinned; the other couldn't reach far enough to touch you. I remember the blurred face of a stranger peering through our shattered window, telling us not to move. I remember wondering if the driver who hit us was okay. But mostly, I remember the absolute terror of the silence between my gasps for air, a silence where I couldn't hear your breathing.

In that mangled Jeep, while we waited for the sirens, we made a pact. I was panicked, gasping for air against the steering wheel, but you were the brave one that day."Tim, honey, are you hurt? I think I'm going to die. I can't breathe," I whispered. "I think I'm okay," you croaked. Your voice was shaking, but fiercely defiant. "No, Mom. You aren't going to die. We're going to make it out of here."

When the paramedics finally arrived after what felt like an eternity, the heavy crunch of their tools pried the door open. As they reached in for me, I pleaded with them: "Him first. Please, take care of my son first." I didn't care about my crushed arm or the blinding pain in my ankle. I only cared that you were breathing. "Oh, Lord Jesus!" I cried out as they loaded me into the ambulance, separating us in the midst of the chaos. I didn't know then that we would both make it out alive. We didn't perish in that wreckage. God sent His angels; He still has a plan for us.

Love,

Mom

The Recovery, Anger, and Guilt

The days following the crash were a blur of sterile white walls, the rhythmic beeping of monitors, and the searing pain of physical reconstruction. I lay immobilized in a bed at OhioHealth Mansfield Hospital. Metal plates, screws, and desperate prayers had painstakingly put my right arm and right ankle back together. But the physical agony paled in comparison to the emotional one. Timothy was airlifted to the Children's Hospital in Columbus on the very day of the accident, sustaining a liver laceration and a broken knee. Being separated from my son while we were both suffering felt like a cruel, secondary wound.

In the middle of this nightmare, Jim, my husband, became our silent anchor. He was a weary traveler dividing his soul and his time. Every day, he managed the daily operations of our family business, Spruce Hill Inn and Cottages. Then, he would race along the highway to tend to me before driving even further south to sit by Timothy's bed. We were no longer just a family in recovery; we were a family divided by geography and pain. Everything will get back to normal soon. We just have to heal and wait, I told myself as I stared at the blank hospital ceiling.

LETTER 2: The Longest Twenty-Two Days

October 18, 2017, Spruce Hill, Cottage 119/120

Dearest Timothy,

It's been 22 days since the accident, and we are finally home. Coming back from the hospital to the quiet of Spruce Hill, our sanctuary of rustic cottages tucked away in the rolling, wooded hills, should feel like a relief. But yesterday, I painstakingly hobbled next door to your room, only to watch you turn away from me.

Seeing you so thin, so quiet, and so helpless in your bed is agonizing. I saw the anger in your eyes when you told me to "go away." It felt like a knife twisting in my chest. I know you are in physical and emotional pain, but it stung because, deep down, I feel I deserve it. I feel like I failed at my only job: keeping you safe. I was the one driving. I was supposed to be the one to protect you.

The violence of the crash did something to us. It didn't just break our bones; it shattered our sense of safety in the world. I'd do anything to change that Wednesday morning. I'd keep us home. I'd never have turned the key in the ignition. Anything but this.

But we are here. We survived. And I am praying for the Lord to wrap us both in His comfort as we navigate this long, dark storm together.

Love,

Mom

The Ghost in the Passenger Seat

The scars on my arm have faded to silver, but the scars on my soul still throb whenever I watch Timothy struggle. For a long time after Jim brought us home, I thought the "miracle" was simply that we were alive. Everyone at church talked about our survival as a profound miracle and prayed earnestly for our swift recovery. But as Tim and I navigated the endless pain, the countless doctor appointments, and the grueling physical rehab, something fundamental shifted. We survived the wreckage, but somewhere in the blur of all that medical chaos, we lost our sweet connection to each other.

The trauma had planted a deep seed of hyper-vigilance inside me. Because I had almost lost him in a split second, I spent the next weeks and months trying to micromanage his life. I became a "Lawnmower Parent," the kind of mother who frantically runs ahead of her child, trying to mow down every obstacle so he never has to experience a single bump or scrape. When he finally went back to school, I hovered over his every assignment. I stepped in to negotiate with his teachers to reduce his stress.

The accident had frozen him in time. Before the crash, he was a vibrant teenager with big plans. Hoping for a fresh start, he asked to transfer to a public school the following year. But while he managed to push his way through to graduation, the spark in his eyes was extinguished. He skipped his prom, and the joyful launch into adulthood I had pictured never happened.

Today, he is only willing to drive the work truck around the private, perfectly safe roads of Spruce Hill. To him, the open highway represents the terrifying unknown, the exact place where control is violently snatched away. His refusal to get a driver's license is fear, a deep-seated trauma. It infected his entire view of the future, shutting down any desire to pursue college or build a life beyond our property lines.

I convinced myself this was just a season, perhaps a gap year or two, to let his mind heal. But two years bled into three, and three quietly stretched into four. As the calendar pages turned, my well of empathy slowly curdled into resentment. I was raised in the Philippines, where education wasn't an expectation; it was a rare, hard-fought privilege.

I vividly remembered sitting in crowded classrooms with shared textbooks, desperate for just a sliver of a chance to succeed. Looking at my son now, surrounded by boundless American opportunity, and watching him refuse to even reach out his hand, bred a maddening, suffocating powerlessness.

Psalm 127:4-5 (KJV) says: "As arrows are in the hand of a mighty man, so are children of the youth. Happy is the man that hath his quiver full of them." But our quiver wasn't full of arrows; it held just one. And when you only have one arrow, you obsess over how straight it is. You hyper-focus on the fletching, the sharpness, and the preparation. You spend every ounce of your energy ensuring it is perfectly ready for flight. There is a distinct, suffocating grief in spending the first fourteen years of your child's life perfectly carving an arrow, only to endure a car crash and spend the next nine years watching that arrow stay stuck in the dirt.

LETTER 3: The Prophecy and the Archer

August 28, 2022, The Front Porch

Dearest Timothy,

I don't know if I've ever fully shared the weight your name carries. It means "Honoring God" or "God's Coworker." To Dad and me, you weren't just a son; you were the ministry we were called to. You were not just born, you were awaited against all odds. Your Dad and I met and married later; I was in my late thirties, and he was in his mid-fifties. We had already made peace with the quiet, assuming the window for a family had stayed shut. We were prepared to find other ways to nurture the world.

Then, there was you.

Everything shifted the moment we knew you were coming. Your Dad looked at the miracle of you and knew his assignment from the Lord had changed. He set aside the full-time training and service in Anaheim to build a life here. We didn't travel for the gospel; we stayed to raise you, our one "miracle boy," as our offering to Him.

As the heavy silence of your trauma settled over our house, I found myself digging through old boxes, desperate for a lifeline. I found my dusty journals from your infancy. My fingers trembled over the faded ink where I had written: "Lord, I know You have given us this boy for Your purpose. I can already see a bold leader's spirit in him. He is going to carry Your light so far." Reading those words broke me. I needed to remind myself, and you, that your life didn't begin with a scream of metal in a Jeep; it began with a divine call.

Maybe that's why the current stillness hurts so much. When I see you sitting on the couch, refusing to launch, anchored to the glow of a computer screen instead of the world waiting for you, my heart fractures. You have the velocity for flight, but it feels like my only arrow has fallen into the dirt, and you are content to stay there. I came across Kahlil Gibran's poem recently, and his words pierced through my frustration:

You are the bows from which your children, as living arrows, are sent forth. The Archer sees the mark upon the path of the infinite, and He bends you with His might that His arrows may go swift and far. Let your bending in the

Archer's hand be for gladness; for even as He loves the arrow that flies, so He loves also the bow that is stable.[1]

Today, I am praying for the grace to be that stable bow, even when the arrow feels stuck. I am asking the Archer to take the tension out of my grip and place it back into His hands. God's prophecies for your life don't expire just because the timeline gets messy. You are still Timothy. You are still His.

Love,

Mom

The Idolatry of the Syllabus

For years, I treated Christian parenting like a spiritual formula: I believed that if I provided the right inputs -Christian school, youth group, piano lessons, perfectly curated environments- God would guarantee the right outputs. I had turned my theology into a syllabus. When our children flourish, we humbly attribute it to the Lord's mercy and do not claim our own merit. When they go astray or stagnate, we are quick to take the blame.

Sitting on the front porch of the Manor house, watching the rhythmic back-and-forth of Timothy mowing the lawn, I was haunted by a ghost of a question: Is the Lord visiting the sins of my past upon my child? In my remorse, I cried out for His grace, begging Him to spare Timothy from my mistakes and to reach his heart where I could not.

This exact, crushing weight of secret self-blame fueled my frantic need to control his timeline. If I could just push him into college, if I could just force him to succeed, it would prove that I hadn't ruined him.

Drawing on the teachings of Witness Lee, a prominent 20th-century Chinese Christian teacher, my perspective shifted entirely. I realized there is a profound difference between mere patience and true long-suffering. As Lee writes, "Patience is toward circumstances, matters, and things, whereas long suffering is toward persons."[2] You need patience for things. You need it when waiting in a long grocery store line or waiting for a package to arrive.

But long-suffering is for people. Long-suffering is the agonizing, beautiful grace required to wait for a human soul to awaken. It is enduring the friction of a relationship without trying to force the outcome. I had been demanding that God resurrect my broken dreams for my child, but God was asking me to practice the long-suffering required for Timothy to awaken to his own God-given dreams.

LETTER 4: The Grace of Long-Suffering

July 18, 2023, The Manor Front Porch

Dearest Timothy,

I think I am finally beginning to understand God's "frustration" with man. He desires His life to be expressed through us, yet He honors the gift of free will, even when we use it to stand still. I feel that same agonizing tension every day. If I could step inside your skin and navigate this path for you, I would. I would lift you out of this frozen moment and carry you toward the horizon, desperate for you to see the beauty of the life that belongs to you.

When you were small, my patience was physical. It was slowing my pace to match your toddling steps. It was the quiet endurance of sleepless nights, holding you through a fever, or scratching your back until your breathing went deep and rhythmic in sleep. It was waiting for you to tie your shoes, knowing we were late, but letting you find the knot.

Now that you are twenty-three, my patience has moved inward. It has become the grueling discipline of biting my tongue when I want to offer advice you didn't ask for. It is the trembling strength required to stand back and watch you navigate your own maze, even when I am certain I can see the exit. I used to think I just needed patience to fix the silence between us. I realize now that I need something much deeper. I need long-suffering to love you as you are. Long-suffering is the capacity to be misunderstood, to be pushed away, and to still hold the door wide open.

I know things are strained. I know my anxiety must feel like a weight on you. But I want you to know that my love isn't conditional on your achievements or your "launch." I am here. I am not going anywhere. I have finally learned that while I cannot force the spring to come, I can sit with you in the winter. I have time. We have time. I trust that the God who pulled us both from that wreckage is still holding the pen and is not finished with your story.

Love,

Mom

The Shadow of the Sampaguita

In September 2024, the heavy silence in our home in Mansfield, Ohio, collided with a different kind of silence from across the ocean. My niece, Jirehel, Timothy's cousin in the Philippines, was losing her battle with sarcoma, a rare, complex cancer developing in connective tissues like bones, muscles, and blood vessels. The contrast was a jagged pill to swallow: Timothy, healthy but stationary, and Jirehel, dying but running at full tilt. From her hospital bed, she earned her degree with honors, a Cum Laude graduate who was too ill to even attend her own ceremony.

She had dreams of Bible school in Malabon, a life in the States, a husband, and children—dreams that were being snatched away, frame by agonizing frame. I realized then that Jirehel was like the Sampaguita, the white jasmine of our home. It is a bloom that is often most fragrant when it is bruised. Her season was tragically brief, but like that flower, the sweetness of her life lingers in the air long after the petals have fallen.

They exchanged letters in those final weeks. Her words were a stinging contrast to the spirit of stagnation that had settled over my son, yet they were filled with a profound tenderness that only the dying can offer. When she passed, she left behind a massive void and a challenge.

Timothy didn't say much when the news arrived. He didn't erupt in tears or offer a eulogy. Instead, he became a shadow. I watched him through the Manor's window, his pace with the lawnmower slowed, and his eyes fixed on the horizon as if he were looking for a sign from a cousin who was no longer there.

He kept her letters. I saw them once, tucked near his computer, the blue glow of his screen reflecting off the paper where she had written about her "dreams of the US." It was a cruel contrast: the girl who worked so hard for everything and was gone, and the boy who had everything handed to him and wanted nothing at all.

For a moment, I thought the grief would be a catalyst, a turning point. I thought he would stand up, grab his keys, and declare that he was ready to live the life she couldn't. But instead of launching, he retreated further. He grew his hair longer, hiding his face like a veil. I realized then that I couldn't shame him into purpose. Even the memory of Jirehel, as powerful as it was, couldn't break the seal on his heart. Only God could do that.

LETTER 5: The Life She Didn't Get to Live

October 5, 2024, Spruce Hill Turtle Pond

Dearest Timothy,

I've been rereading the messages Jirehel sent you before she passed. I can't stop thinking about that one line: "I'm young, I have dreams, and I like to visit the US someday." She wanted the life you're currently taking for granted. She spent her final weeks spitting blood and fighting through the haze of fentanyl patches, yet she was "joyful" to have earned her degree. She studied in the dark of a hospital ward, while you sit in the light of a country lodge with every resource at your fingertips.

You, too, are young. And don't you have dreams? I close my eyes, and I see the boy you used to be. I see the little boy who stood tall in the kitchen, chest puffed out, telling me, "Mom, I'm going to be a doctor." My heart had soared. It was my own childhood dream, resurrected in you. I imagined the white coat. I imagined the healing hands. I imagined the legacy you would carry into the world. I open my eyes, and the physician is gone. In his place is a young man who sits idle, thinking college is a waste of money. But what is the cost of a stagnant soul?

When I look at you now, I don't just see my son. I see the cousin who reached out to you. I see the girl who finished college from a bed because she refused to let cancer take her mind before it took her body. When you sit at your computer or look out at the hills, do you ever feel her presence? Do you ever feel the weight of the life she didn't get to live?

You are her legacy now. Every time you refuse to drive, every time you say college is a scam, every time you retreat into the blue glow of a screen, it feels like a second death for Jirehel. I am not asking you to live for her. I am asking you to honor the breath you still have, the breath she was fighting for until the very end. Don't just survive. Live the life she didn't get to.

Love,

Mom

The Breaking Point on the Stairs

In the spiritual warfare over our son's soul, Jim was a patient diplomat, willing to quietly wait out the siege. But I was done waiting. I wanted to play the warring tiger mother. I wanted to storm the gates, shatter the walls of trauma holding Timothy captive, and forcefully change the trajectory of his life. I was walking down the hallway, and Timothy's bedroom door was wide open. I looked inside and saw the overwhelming mess of his stagnation: dirty glasses, stacked plates, a line of soda cans, an unmade bed, and the blue glow of the monitor illuminating his face as he played his games, completely detached from reality.

Something inside me snapped. Years of hyper-vigilance, suppressed fear, and spiritual exhaustion boiled over in an instant. I marched into his room and exploded. We had a massive, deafening argument. I yelled that I hadn't given birth to him just to watch him waste his life playing video games. In my blind, fleshly frustration, my fear morphed into physical rage. I grabbed a laundry basket with his dirty clothes and threw it across the room. It slammed into the wall with a sharp crack. Timothy stood up immediately. He reached out, firmly grabbed my hands to stop the chaos, and shouted, "Mom, please stop!" In the frantic struggle of my flailing, my fingernails raked across his skin. Blood welled up and dripped down his arm.

The sight of his blood broke me. The anger instantly drained out of my body, leaving only a hollow, crushing guilt. I pulled away, walked out to the staircase, sat down on the steps, and buried my face in my hands. I wept for ten solid minutes. I wept for the accident, for the wasted years, and for the ugly, controlling monster my own fear had turned me into.

Then, I heard movement. Timothy walked out of his room, his arms full of the dirty dishes and cups. He walked right past me on the stairs, took them to the kitchen, and loaded them into the dishwasher. Then, he went back and started cleaning his room. A few minutes later, he passed by me on the stairs again. He didn't say a word. He didn't demand an apology or yell at me for his bleeding arm. He just paused, gently rubbed my back, and kept walking.

As I sat there in the quiet aftermath, the Holy Spirit gently broke me. Through my tears, the words of Ephesians 6:12 washed over my mind: "For we wrestle not against flesh and blood, but against principalities, against powers, against the rulers of the darkness of this world, against spiritual wickedness in high places." The realization was a physical blow. I was literally wrestling with my son. I was so exhausted because I was fighting the wrong enemy. I had to stop fighting against him and start fighting for him in high places.

LETTER 6: The Apology on the Stairs

January 7, 2026. The Country Lodge Kitchen

Dearest Timothy,

My heart has been so heavy since our fight today, and I haven't been able to find peace. I am writing this first and foremost to ask for your forgiveness. In my moment of anger and frustration, I crossed a line. There is no excuse for throwing things, and I am deeply sorry for hurting you physically and scratching your arm when you tried to stop me. It was wrong of me, and I regret it more than I can say.

When I told you that I didn't give birth to you just to play computer games, it came out as an attack, but it was born from a place of deep love. I believe you have such a high purpose in this life. I see so much potential in you, and because I love you so fiercely, I get terrified when I see you stuck.

Dad and I spend so much time on our knees before the Lord, crying out and asking how to help you. But sometimes, my fear for your future masks itself as anger in the present.

I don't want to push you away; I want to be your biggest encourager. You are turning twenty-three soon, and you have so much to offer this world.

By the way... thank you for the rub on the back you gave me while I was crying on the stairs. Even though you didn't say anything, it meant everything to me. Underneath it all, you are still my sweet, loving boy.

Love,

Mom

Active Trust: The Rails of Prayer

My breakdown on the stairs proved I could not force change through my own strength. There had to be a better way to fight for my son. In my search for how to fight this new kind of battle, I found myself drawn to the legacy of mothers who had gone before me. I read about Saint Monica of the 4th century, known as the 'Persistent Mother.' She spent decades praying, weeping, and storming heaven for her rebellious, wandering son, Augustine, until a bishop famously comforted her with the words: "Go your way; as you live, it cannot be that the son of these tears should perish."[3] I also read about Hudson Taylor's mother, who locked herself in a room and refused to emerge until she felt the absolute assurance of her cynical teenager's salvation, praying him into the Kingdom at the exact moment he surrendered miles away. Reading their stories, a profound distinction clicked into place for me: These women didn't nag; they prayed and fought.

It was also during this time that I discovered the writings of the 17th-century Christian mystic, Madame Guyon. She spoke of a deeper state of surrender, a state where we stop looking at the person who frustrates us and start looking only at the Hand that permits the trial. She wrote, "I saw that it was the hand of God that struck me, and not the hand of the creature."[4] She taught that to the soul entirely resigned to God, "everything is a remedy." Reading those words, a hard truth pierced my heart: my frustration was actually a rebellion against the remedy God was using in my own life. I had to move from wanting Timothy to change for his sake to being willing to let God change me through the waiting.

Sitting in the quiet of the lodge, I opened the *Life-study of Philippians.* In it, Witness Lee describes a level of forbearance that completely surpasses human effort. He explains that we often try to force ourselves to be patient, acting like a lamp trying to burn without any oil. We exhaust ourselves, the wick eventually chars, and we are left completely burned out in resentment. The only remedy is letting Christ live through us. Lee wrote: "Our forbearance should be Christ Himself... we do not have such a life in ourselves. We must enjoy the Lord as our supply."[5]

Watchman Nee, a devoted minister who learned the true cost of complete surrender and spent the last twenty years of his life in a Chinese prison for his faith, captured this beautifully. He said, "Our prayers are like laying the track for the train. The locomotive has great power and can run thousands of miles a day. But if there is no track, it cannot move a single inch."[6] I also remembered that this same principle of surrender applies to our expectations.

Franklin Graham, the son of the great evangelist Billy Graham, rebelled. He loved guns, motorcycles, and independence. He wanted nothing to do with his father's legacy. He famously shot up a riverbank with a semi-automatic weapon while his father prepared for a crusade. In his autobiography, *Rebel with a Cause*, Franklin recounts the exact moment his father finally confronted his rebellion in a hotel room in Switzerland just before his 22nd birthday. Billy Graham didn't yell, beg, or try to control him. He simply told him the truth and left the choice in his hands. He quotes his father saying, "You can't continue to play the middle ground. Either you're going to choose to follow and obey Him or reject Him."[7] Just days later, alone in a hotel room in Jerusalem, Franklin finally surrendered his life to Christ, writing: "The rebel had found the cause." God took that rebellious, gun-loving spirit and redeemed it. Franklin didn't just return; he took the baton, leading Samaritan's Purse into war zones that only a man with a warrior's spirit could handle.

LETTER 7: The Song I'm Waiting For

January 12, 2026. The Lodge Hallway

Dearest Timothy,

I passed by your room last night and heard the song you were playing. A worldly mainstream song. I headed to your bathroom to clean it, and I remembered a different sound. Do you know what your first word was and where you spoke it? You were just a baby then, not even a year old yet. I was holding you in my arms. Your dad and I were attending the Lord's Table Meeting in Anaheim, and the whole church was singing Hymn #551: "I've believed the true report,

Hallelujah to the Lamb! Hallelujah. Hallelujah!"[8] And then, exactly at that interval before we could sing the next line, you shouted, "Hallelujah!" It rang out clear and loud. All the brothers and sisters around us were startled, then they looked at you and burst into laughter. It was pure joy. Your first contribution to the world wasn't a cry; it was a praise.

I know you don't want to go to church meetings and conferences right now, even though you were a church kid who sang Bible songs, read, and recited the Scriptures. I am holding onto that memory. You can listen to your music for now. You can grow your hair long. But I know who you are. You are the boy who shouted Hallelujah before he could even walk. That praise is still in your DNA. I'll be here when the music changes.

Love,

Mom

The Vision in the Lobby

The weight of my anxiety often feels like a physical thing, a heavy coat I wear even in the heat of summer. But occasionally, God gives us a glimpse of what it looks like to take off the coat.

On January 29, 2026, I traveled to Charlotte, North Carolina, for a hope*story Conference. I needed to be in a room of people who believed that stories could be redeemed, because my own story felt stuck in a loop of silence and slammed doors. I wandered through a sea of merchandise, tables overflowing with new books and nice souvenirs. I found myself drawn to a display blooming with vibrant floral designs: it was Ruth Chou Simons's table. Although the looming storm forced us to leave before I could hear her keynote, I couldn't walk away without a copy of one of her books. As I handed my card to the handsome young man managing the table, I felt a nudge of curiosity.

"Are you Ruth's son?" I asked.

"Yes," he replied with a smile.

In that instant, the conference lobby faded away. A vivid, clear vision flashed before me: my own son, Timothy, standing behind a table piled with my books, handing out copies of "Letters to Timothy." Was it a daydream, or a divine glimpse into the future? The weight of it hit me all at once. Overwhelmed by a sense of hope and calling, I stepped into the corner, wiped away my tears, and captured a few photos of Ruth's son, a quiet tribute to the legacy I now believe I am writing. I realized then: I am not writing these letters to the boy in the bedroom. I am writing to the new man at the table.

Chapter 9

Patience in Daily Life: Needing Patience in the Everyday

By Cathy Smith

As I sat looking at his phone on our bed, I was shaking all over. Mad, upset, and hurt after reading the images and text messages I had just seen on his phone. Why? Why is he doing this? To us, to our family? I felt like Caesar being stabbed in the back.

Life throws trials our way as we do life, and we do the best we can. Was I perfect? Heck no, I know that. How we treat others, and especially the ones we love, shows our character & what we hold as our standards.

I loved my husband very much, so much that I was able to forgive him after the first act of infidelity. I honestly thought that was going to take me out, but by God's grace, I was able to forgive. We had two small children when the first betrayal occurred, and I was thinking of them. I didn't want them passed back and forth like a football. I also didn't know all the information I do now.

It has taken so much time and patience to try to understand all that has happened in the past. And I still don't understand it all, but there is a point you reach where you realize that you probably will never understand all of what happened to you and why. You realize that you simply have to move forward with your life.

In the days after the divorce, when I was crying uncontrollably, I never thought I would get to a point where I was okay. Okay to move forward with my life and on my own. It can be a scary thing to feel and do, but you know you have to take that next step, whether you want to or not. Getting a divorce (something I never wanted to do or thought would happen) has taught me that there are times in our lives when we have to be patient, whether we want to be or not. Having to deal with lawyers, dividing everything up, and learning a new way to live requires patience. The definition of patience is the capacity to accept or tolerate delay, trouble, or suffering without getting angry or upset. Now I am not going to say I was never upset or angry during the divorce because I was. I have learned a great deal from this process. I have learned not only to be patient during the process of trials but also in the everyday tasks of life.

I believe patience is needed every day in some form. That patience level can be different from day to day. Whether it is being patient with others or even with myself, I believe it is something we all need to work on. Patience can also go alongside the other fruit of the Spirit as well.

There may be days I need patience, self-control, and love, while on another day it could be a different kind of combination of the fruit of the Spirit. Some days we need more patience than other days; it just depends on what we are going through at that time.

I can be impatient with wanting to know certain things right away, such as knowing what a health test result might mean, passing an exam at school, or having patience with a screaming child in a grocery store. There are so many incidents that happen in our everyday lives, and our lives are constantly changing.

Learning patience over the years has definitely been a struggle for me, and I am sure it's an endeavor for many as well. Having to wait on **His** timing versus ours can be extremely difficult. With the fast pace of the world and everyone wanting to have the answers now, it is hard to be patient. But there are plenty of times in our lives where we simply have to be patient and wait; there is no other thing we can do. We have to remember that waiting patiently shows that we trust in God's timing and power. "Be still in the presence of the Lord, and wait patiently for him to act. Don't worry about evil people who prosper or fret about their wicked schemes" (Psalm 37:7, NLT). I have had to wait years to finally feel calm within myself. Being in a marriage where I had to walk on eggshells constantly was difficult, and it took an emotional & mental toll on me. When someone you thought was supposed to love you for the rest of your life turns into someone you don't even know anymore in your marriage, and the words he speaks and yells at you are so hurtful and unbelievable, it can take a real toll on your life. I believe it also caused me issues with my health.

I remember having to wait to know what my first child was. The doctor didn't let me take a test to find out what I was going to have, so I had to wait until my child was born to know whether it was a boy or a girl. That waiting drove me a bit nuts. There were times I thought, *No, this will be a nice surprise for me and everyone else to wait and then have it be a big hooray at the time of the birth.* And then other times I was like, *I just wish I knew what I was having, so this way I could plan and prepare.* A great many items I received for my first baby shower were yellow and other neutral colors, which was fine, but at the same time, I would have liked to have known. I needed months of patience as I awaited the birth of my first child. I was so excited to find out that it was a boy! For some reason, deep down, I was hoping for a boy, and the love, patience, joy, goodness, peace, faithfulness, and self-control it took to have him made it all worth the wait.

In the waiting, we need to remember that God will fulfill His promises ...we only need to be patient. He knows everything better than we could even imagine. We need to remember that God knows it all. It is unfathomable for us humans to grasp this. To know everything, everyone, every event for all of time is so hard for our minds to understand. Everything that is done in secret, every word that is spoken, every action that has been taken and will be taken, the seasons of everyone's life, and what happens to all the animals of this world - He knows about everything! God knows it all, and that is truly amazing. We cannot do what He does. We cannot think as He does, and it is even said in Isaiah 55:8-9 (NLT): "My thoughts are nothing like your thoughts," says the Lord. "And my ways are far beyond anything you could imagine. For just as the heavens are higher than the earth, so my ways are higher than your ways and my thoughts higher than your thoughts."

In the waiting, we learn to persevere, endure, and trust in His timing, not ours. I think that is the biggest part we need to realize. We need to grasp that God knows what is best for us, and even though it may feel like forever for us, we must wait on his timing. Some people may only have to wait a little while, while others may have to wait years for an answer or a result. Is it fair? Who am I to say? I do not know what the future holds for every single person on this planet. That is only for God to know and deal with. God knows each of our hearts, minds, and souls. He knows us better than we do. He knows what each one of us needs, even if we don't comprehend it.

There are ample situations in this world that can cause us not to endure through the hard times. Life can wear us down slowly, bit by bit, day by day, until we hit rock bottom. However, we need to be strong and remind ourselves every day that God knows best, and we need to press forward and rely on Him for the help and endurance we need to get through the situation we are facing. Don't let your guard down, stay on the course, and ask for His help every moment of every day if you have to. Just don't give up!

As I have said, my divorce has got to be the number one thing that has really made me struggle. There were days I just wanted to do nothing but watch TV all day; I just wanted to crawl onto my couch and do absolutely nothing. But life doesn't let you do that. There are jobs you have to go to, bills that still need to be paid, appointments to keep, home repairs to make, meals to cook, and the list goes on. You don't feel like it, but you have to keep getting up every day, get dressed, and keep moving onward, whether you like it or not.

I would smile when I didn't want to smile, trying to get through the mundane events of life. It took plenty of my energy and patience. I knew trying to rush through my emotions would not produce a good outcome for me in the long run. Slow and steady wins the race, and I am still on this path. I know it is going to take patience and time to move forward and achieve the positive results I would like. Sure, I would love the microwave effect, where everything is fixed ASAP, but that is not realistic or real life. We are all different, and how we deal with and process information is different for all of us. Some of us may move faster than others.

There is nothing wrong with asking others for help. If you need prayer, ask for it. Have others pray for you or the situation that you are going through. When people come together and help one another, it can help us in so many ways. It creates a ripple effect that comforts the receiver and the giver in a unique way. I had to ask my family and friends for prayer before, during & after my divorce. I am so glad I did. It helped me tremendously! Knowing that you are not alone and that people of like mind are caring for you is comforting.

Here are a few quotes that have helped me in my journey:

"When we get together, I want to encourage you in your faith, but I also want to be encouraged by yours." Romans 1:12, NLT

Frederick Douglass's most famous quote is "If there is no struggle there is no progress," which emphasizes that growth and change require effort, agitation, and perseverance.[1]

Stephen Chbosky wrote, "...things change. And friends leave. And life doesn't stop for anybody."[2]

I have realized through my divorce and the betrayals that I have had to deal with that pain is like a teacher, and through pain we grow and learn. Our personal growth comes from being forced to confront, adapt, and learn from life's challenges, even though we would rather not learn the hard way. Life doesn't stop for anybody, and even though it may be nice to have it stop for a while, so that we can get a grasp on the situation. It will not stop. We must move forward and have the endurance to be patient.

People by no means need to go through something painful to learn that we need patience. We can learn it through a great many other situations as well. As I have said earlier, waiting to find out what I was having during my pregnancy was not a troubling situation, but the waiting, the not knowing of how to prepare for the baby, was hard. Patience is a spiritual discipline that often involves enduring the trials and difficulties of life. It's not just passive waiting we must do; it's active endurance that involves self-control, hope, and compassion. It means being able to bear wrongs without getting upset so easily, to withstand the hardship, and not retaliate so quickly.

Remember, we all face obstacles in our lives; no one can go through life without dealing with some kind of issue. How we deal with these issues shows our character to others and even to ourselves. Controlling our emotions does not mean we don't have any emotions. It simply means that we can keep our composure during a crisis.

Now, I will admit that I have lost my cool during spats with others. I believe we all have at one time or another. Especially when I was younger. I didn't understand how my actions could make others feel. Or perhaps how I made things worse. It has taken time and trial and error to learn how to handle these situations over the years. And this has been a road I learned from, and I have needed much patience not only with others but also with myself.

During an argument with another person, it can be a heated time with emotions running high. Perhaps there has been a buildup of emotions, running high within you or the other person, and, like a volcano, the situation blows up! When emotions are high and words are flying out of our mouths, it is hard to remain calm and overlook any offenses that may have been said. Some people are very good at articulating their thoughts during a disagreement, while others have a harder time figuring it out. It may be best if the person who has a harder time speaking during the disagreement asks for a so-called time-out for a bit, so they can really think about what is being said and how to respond. Again, not every dispute will allow time to do this, so you will have to think about how best to resolve the matter as quickly and with as much wisdom as possible. My three points for you on a disagreement would be:

1. STOP: Think about the situation and breathe. Don't act instantly

2. THINK: Is my reaction showing patience? Or is it showing a need for power?

3. SURRENDER: Choose to trust that patience leads to a better outcome than a forced power.

Remember that God is always there for you; you can call out to him no matter when or where you are. Ask for his help, ask for his patience, his guidance in times of trouble. This reminds me of Ephesians 4:2 (NLT), where it says, "Always be humble and gentle. Be patient with each other, making allowance for each other's faults because of your love." Also, Proverbs 15:18 (NLT) says, "A hot-tempered person starts fights; a cool-tempered person stops them."

People's circumstances can be similar or completely different. How we respond reveals our character to ourselves and to others. I believe that almost everyone, if not everyone, wants respect, kindness, love, understanding, forgiveness, gentleness, joy, peace, faithfulness, patience, and self-control. If we each want these things for ourselves, doesn't that mean others want them for themselves too? In Proverbs 14:17 (NLT), it says, "Short-tempered people do foolish things, and schemers are hated." In Proverbs 14:29 (NLT), it says, "People with understanding control their anger; a hot temper shows great foolishness." And in Proverbs 16:32, it states, "Better to be patient than powerful; better to have self-control than to conquer a city."

How will you choose to handle your next intense situation when it arises? Will you fly off the handle with an outburst of some kind? Or will you do your best to remain calm? Assess the situation the best you can and act accordingly. Will you show patience? Love? understanding? Will you remember to stop, breathe, and think about the situation before reacting so quickly? Sometimes I have thought about arguments I have had in the past, and there have been times when I wish I could have gone back and changed what I said or how I said it. Unfortunately, we can't go back in time. That's why, if you know of a conflict that may arise in the future, it would be best to think about how you are going to talk about it.

However, most conflicts erupt on the spot, and words get said that perhaps should not have been spoken. Do your very best to be proactive with a situation if at all possible, and if not, remember to take the time you need to process the situation before you speak. As my children have learned, it is hard to put the toothpaste back into the tube after you have already squeezed it out. To close, I'll quote one more verse to recall the golden rule in Matthew 7:12: "Do to others whatever you would like them to do to you. This is the essence of all that is taught in the law and the prophets." So how would you like to be treated?

Live each day with love, joy, peace, patience, goodness, faithfulness, gentleness, and self-control. We are only given a certain amount of time here; let us make our lives the best we can.

In times of having to wait, here are some steps to remember:

- Take a deep breath or even a few deep breaths to calm yourself. (Stop for a few moments and simply breathe.)

- Pray. Yes, God already knows what you need, but he wants that relationship with you. Go to Him for help, ask Him for what you need, and thank Him as well for being there for you- just like you would a friend.

- Remember Jesus and think, "What would He do at a time like this?" (Be Christ-like. Imitate Christ's endurance)

- Remember that God's schedule is something we cannot see & won't understand. Therefore, we must trust Him. Even though it may be hard.

- Trust that God will give you patience and understanding for the next step that needs to take place.

- Study Scripture.

- Remember to stay strong and persevere forward.

- If you need to apologize for losing your patience, then do so. We can all lash out at others in times of frustration. It's ok to be sorry, just let the other person or persons know that.

*

About the
Authors

Dr. Tyann Beenken, DPT

Tyann is a farm wife, homeschool mom of four, and a physical therapist. She has recently stepped away from private practice and into writing to share honest, heartfelt words about faith, motherhood, wellness, and letting go of career expectations. Her prayer is that her words would point people back to Christ and to the true peace and purpose found in quiet surrender and obedience.

Website: www.movedbeyondwellness.com

https://www.tyannbeenken.com

Facebook: https://facebook.com/movedbeyondwellness;

Stephanie A. Genrich

After three decades of working in advertising and marketing, Stephanie Genrich has returned to her first love - writing. Upon graduating with a B.A. in Journalism from Indiana University, Stephanie immediately headed west, where she worked in Los Angeles for several years before traveling the world and finally landing in Indianapolis, Indiana, where she lives with her husband, two children, two Golden Retrievers, and one rather large, annoying cat.

Website: www.stephaniegenrich.com

Facebook: https://www.facebook.com/stephanie.genrich.58

Marilynn Lester

Marilynn taught in public schools for six years, after which she became director of a church-run preschool. She loves music, teaching, traveling, and writing, and is thankful to God for the opportunity to experience it all. She and her husband ministered on numerous mission trips to Russia, Ukraine, Paraguay, Ecuador, and Spain, visiting many of those locations more than once. Family time means spending time with her husband, two sons, and daughters-in-law, five grandchildren (and their spouses), and four great-grandchildren. She is currently working on a historical fiction novel based on her ancestors' journey from Prussia to Southern Russia/Ukraine.

Website: www.marilynn-lester.com

Facebook: www.facebook.com/marilynnlesterauthor/

Lisa Recor

isa M. Recor is a Christian writer and published poet, best known for *From Broken to Believer: A Collection of Poetry & Scripture*. With more than 25 years of experience in Sales and Marketing, she brings both professional insight and heartfelt authenticity to her writing. Lisa is passionate about sharing messages of faith, restoration, and hope through the written word. She currently resides in Morgantown, Kentucky, with her husband. Together, they cherish their four children and eight grandchildren. When she's not writing or reading, Lisa enjoys walking, crafting, and spending time outdoors, drawing inspiration from God's creation for her work and daily life.

Website: www.suchatimeasthis.net/

Instagram: www.instagram.com/lisa_m_recor/

Facebook: www.facebook.com/suchatimeasthisblog2023

www.facebook.com/lmsmith2966/

Kathleen R Fischer

Kathleen is a devoted mom to three adult children and a fur mom to our service dog Bugsy. She is a retired private home care provider. She now lives in North Phoenix along the foothills.

Email: krfischer2018@gmail.com

Instagram: www.instagram.com/kathleenfischer2017/

Kelly Higdon

Kelly has been a Christ follower since she was 15. She currently serves as a leader and teacher with the hope*network through her local church and as a member of the Civil Air Patrol Chaplain Corps, serving as a Character Development Instructor. She lives in the beautiful Golden Valley of North Carolina with her airline pilot husband and is sort of an empty nester after a decade of homeschooling her two sons. She enjoys traveling, coffee, and all those lovely conversations that occur between strangers on the way to some other place.

Website:www.substack.com/@kmhwriter

Instagram: www.instagram.com/kelly.m.higdon

Facebook: www.facebook.com/kelly.m.higdon

Jennifer Jackson

Jennifer Jackson is a devout woman of Elohim, wife, mother of three, poet, life coach to women with mother wounds, and author. She enjoys reading, writing, walking, spending time with her family, coaching, and encouraging women to live their lives from a place of healing rather than a place of woundedness and brokenness. She is a lover of truth, integrity, true relationships, cookies, art, chips, turtles, horses, and living life BIG. She truly loves her Heavenly Father, her family, her friends, and her calling in life. Her best life is yet to come, and she is extremely excited about it.

Elizabeth Clark

Elizabeth Clark is a writer, mother, wife, and the co-owner of Spruce Hill Inn and Cottages in Mansfield, Ohio, which she runs alongside her husband, Jim. Raised in the Philippines, she brings a deep appreciation for faith, resilience, and the grace of God into both her hospitality business and her writing. She is passionate about the power of prayer, church history, and finding God's profound presence in difficult seasons of waiting. Beth considers her greatest calling and ministry to be her family, especially her miracle son, Timothy. When she isn't managing the lodge or writing, you can find her on the front porch of the Manor house, praying and enjoying the Lord's presence.

Website: www.sprucehillinn.com,

Email: bethclark@sprucehillinn.com,

Facebook: www.facebook.com/beth.clark.3230/

Cathy Smith

Cathy Smith is a daughter, sister, and a mom of three adult children. She worked faithfully for many years, learning various subjects while homeschooling her three children and helping to run a homeschool co-op, which was a great learning experience for her and her kids. These experiences helped her teach others in areas of her life, such as volunteering and work-related situations. Life has thrown some unexpected situations in her path over the last few years, but she continues to move forward to see what God has in store for her future. During these last few years, she has really had to learn patience, and God is still working on her. She wants to encourage others the best that she can. Life is short, every day is precious, and we all have this one life to live. Let's live our lives to their full potential with as few regrets as possible by following the golden rule: do unto others as you would have them do unto you.

Instagram: https://www.instagram.com/cscre-ates_?igsh=OHB2ZnZyaWNuZm5m&utm_source=qr

Endnotes

Chapter One

1. Myers, Michelle and Phoebus, Somer. *She Works His Way: A Practical Guide for Doing What Matters Most in a Get-Things-Done World*. Bethany House, 2021, pg. 98.

2. Niequist, Shauna. *Present over Perfect Guided Journal: Journey to a Simpler, More Soulful Life.* Zondervan, 2021, pg. 17.

3. Comer, John Mark. *The Ruthless Elimination of Hurry.* Waterbrook, 2019, pg 23.

4. Blackaby, Henry; Blackaby, Richard; King, Claude. *Experiencing God: Knowing and Doing the Will of God* 13-Session Bible Study. LifeWay Press, 2007, pg. 47.

5. Ibed. Blackaby. pg. 108.

6. Ibed. Blackaby. pg. 109.

7. Fuller, Malinda. *Obedience Over Hustle*. Shiloh Run Press, 2019, pg. 167.

8. Ibed. Myers. pg. 47.

9. Ibed. Myers.

Chapter Two

1. Chapman, Steven Curtis, "Steven Curtis Chapman 'Disparately Hopeful' After Death of Daughter", *Good Morning America*, ABC, 14 Dec. 2009

2. *Hague Process | USCIS*, www.uscis.gov/adoption/immigration-through-adoption/hague-process. Accessed 21 Feb. 2026.

Chapter Three

1. Walvoord, John F., *The Holy Spirit*, 1958, Dunham Publishing Company, Findlay, Ohio (Book)

Chapter Four

1. de Sales, Francis. "A Quote by Francis de Sales." *Goodreads*, Goodreads, 2008, www.goodreads.com/quotes/40124-have-patience-with-all-things-but-chiefly-have-patience-with. Accessed 20 Apr. 2026.

Chapter Six

1. Vaughan, Julie Anna and Ken Vaughan. *No Regrets: Caught in the Crossfire of An African Civil War.* Flagstaff: Mortens Moore Publishing LLC, 2017

2. "Be Still, My Soul." *Hymns of the Christian Life*, 1962 revised and enlarged edition, Christian Publication, 1962, 306.

Chapter Eight

1. Kahlil Gibran, *The Prophet* (New York: Alfred A. Knopf, 1923), 18.

2. Witness Lee, *Life-study of Galatians* (Anaheim, CA: Living Stream Ministry, 1984), Message 40.

3. Saint Augustine, *Confessions*, Book III, Chapter 12.

4. Jeanne Guyon, *Autobiography of Madame Guyon* (Chicago: Moody Press, 1897).

5. Witness Lee, *Life-study of Philippians* (Anaheim, CA: Living Stream Ministry, 1984).

6. Watchman Nee, *The Prayer Ministry of the Church* (Anaheim, CA: Living Stream Ministry, 1993), 1.

7. Franklin Graham, *Rebel with a Cause* (Nashville: Thomas Nelson, 1995), 120.

8. Charles P. Jones, *Hymns* (Anaheim, CA: Living Stream Ministry), Hymn 551.

Chapter Nine.

1. Douglass, Frederick. "West India Emancipation." *The Frederick Douglass Papers: Series One: Speeches, Debates, and Interviews*, edited by John W. Blassingame, Yale University Press, 1979.

2. Chbosky, Stephen. *The Perks of Being a Wallflower.* Pocket Books, 1999.

Closing

Dear Reader,

Thank you for reading *Patience: Trusting God's Timing in Every Season!*

I want to take a moment to celebrate the incredible authors who contributed to this meaningful book. They have poured their hearts into discovering, clarifying, and sharing their unique messages—and now, you get to benefit from their hard work and dedication.

At hope*books, we are deeply proud of our authors and are honored to partner with them on this journey. If you've ever considered writing and publishing your book, we invite you to visit hopebooks.com to learn more about our coaching and publishing services. We believe that everyone has a message to share and an audience to serve, and the world needs your hopeful words now more than ever.

Once again, let's take a moment to celebrate the hard work of these authors in bringing *Patience: Trusting God's Timing in Every Season to life.*

Sincerely,

Brian Dixon

Publisher, hope*books

Looking to *connect* with a community of writers?

www.hopewriters.com

The world needs your *hope-filled* words more now than ever before.

Thinking about *writing* your own book?

www.hopebooks.com